IMAGES OF WAR

UNITED STATES MARINE CORPS IN VIETNAM

RARE PHOTOGRAPHS FROM WARTIME ARCHIVES

Michael Green

Pen & Sword
MILITARY

First published in Great Britain in 2020 by
PEN & SWORD MILITARY
An imprint of
Pen & Sword Books Ltd
47 Church Street
Barnsley
South Yorkshire
S70 2AS

ISBN 978-1-52675-123-2

Typeset by Concept, Huddersfield, West Yorkshire HD4 5JL.
Printed and bound in India by Replika Press Pvt. Ltd.

Pen & Sword Books Limited incorporates the imprints of Atlas, Archaeology, Aviation, Discovery, Family History, Fiction, History, Maritime, Military, Military Classics, Politics, Select, Transport, True Crime, Air World, Frontline Publishing, Leo Cooper, Remember When, Seaforth Publishing, The Praetorian Press, Wharncliffe Local History, Wharncliffe Transport, Wharncliffe True Crime and White Owl.

For a complete list of Pen & Sword titles please contact
PEN & SWORD BOOKS LIMITED
47 Church Street, Barnsley, South Yorkshire S70 2AS, England
E-mail: enquiries@pen-and-sword.co.uk
Website: www.pen-and-sword.co.uk

Contents

Dedication

The author dedicates this book to Victor H. Krulak, who served in the Marine Corps from 1934 to 1968. Winner of the Navy Cross during the Second World War, he eventually rose to the rank of lieutenant general and was considered a visionary during his time in service. He died at the age of 95 in December 2008.

Acknowledgements

The bulk of the historical images in this work are from the files of the United States Marine Corps Historical Center and will be credited 'USMC'. As with all published works, authors depend on friends for assistance in reviewing their work and their help is greatly appreciated.

Note to the Reader
Reflecting the Marine Corps' long-term involvement in the Vietnam War versus the confines of the size and format of the books in this series, this work can only present the most cursory examination of the subject matter. For those looking for more detailed information, the author suggests consulting the Marine Corps ten-part historical series on its participation in the conflict that can be downloaded from the internet in PDF format at no cost.

Foreword

When the simmering conflict in Vietnam heated up, US Marine Corps units had operated there since 1962. In accordance with long-standing contingency plans, elements of the 3d Marine Division, supported by squadrons of the 1st Marine Aircraft Wing, deployed from Okinawa bases to a highly-strategic enclave, centred on Da Nang and the existing air base complex, in the north of the Republic of Vietnam. This area had not been chosen by chance: it had a port, independent of Saigon and others to the south; it had beaches; it also commanded defiles in the coastwise road and rail net. Its main and enduring disadvantage was that it was adjacent to some of the most hard-core Viet Cong regions in-country, both south and inland to the west.

On the heels of the 3d Marine Division followed the 1st Marine Division and Marine Aircraft Group-36 from California bases. By the end of the year, almost two-thirds of the combat units of the Marine Corps were thus committed to the Vietnamese war.

Yet even as successes in combat and pacification mounted for the US forces and their allies, the war was being lost. The native Vietnamese government proved unsuited to gaining and sustaining the loyalty and obedience of its population. In the United States, another people grew weary and impatient of the war, amplified on a daily basis on television and in the printed media to the extent that the president chose against re-election and Congress began to apply halters to the war effort.

Michael Green's detailed summary of the Marine Corps campaign in the Vietnam War demonstrates the ebb and flow of the counter-insurgency and limited conventional wars that took place simultaneously in Indochina. This strange war fought under strange circumstances placed great demands upon the US Defense Establishment and no less upon the Marine Corps. Michael has succeeded well in explaining the conduct of the war and how the Corps responded to the changing challenges it posed. The well-chosen illustrations provide succinct insights to the character of the war and of the Marine and Navy personnel who served year after year in its prosecution.

Kenneth W. Estes
Lieutenant Colonel US Marines
Author of *Marines Under Armor* (2000)

Chapter One

The Opening Act (1965)

In early 1965, due to the South Vietnamese government's political and military instability, American President Lyndon Johnson ordered a US Marine Light Anti-aircraft Missile (LAAM) Battalion of 500 men to the Republic of Vietnam (RVN). The worry was fear of an aerial attack by North Vietnamese aircraft. The men and equipment of the Marine LAAM were in place around Da Nang airfield in northern South Vietnam by 16 February 1965.

In late February 1965, President Johnson decided to commit major ground combat forces of the United States armed forces to secure portions of South Vietnam, referred to as 'enclaves'. The aim was to help stabilize the government of South Vietnam and its military forces. The initial choice would be either a US Army airborne brigade or a Marine Expeditionary Brigade (MEB).

Arrival

As an MEB contained the organic logistic element and the US Army airborne brigade did not, the decision was to deploy the Marine unit. Between 8 and 9 March 1965, elements of the 9th Marine Expeditionary Brigade (MEB) arrived in South Vietnam unopposed except for minor sniper fire. They came in by sea and air near the coastal city of Da Nang. Their assigned role was the protection of the Da Nang air base and the already-in-place Marine LAAM in an area encompassing roughly 8 square miles.

The men of the LAAM and the 9th MEB would not be the first Marines in South Vietnam. A single Marine officer had arrived in South Vietnam in 1954 as a liaison to the newly-established United States Military Assistance and Advisory Group (MAAG) to the Republic of Vietnam.

By 1964, the number of Marines in South Vietnam had risen to almost 800 men; most were military advisors. However, included in that number were the personnel of a single Marine Medium Helicopter Squadron (HMM, Helicopter Medium Marine). They had arrived at the Da Nang air base in September 1962 to support the Republic of Vietnam Army, hereafter referred to as the 'ARVN'. In contrast, the US Army had approximately 20,000 advisors in South Vietnam by 1964.

The initial Marine troop contingent of the 9th MEB that arrived at Da Nang consisted of approximately 5,000 men, divided into two infantry battalions and two helicopter squadrons. By the end of April 1965, the 9th MEB had around 9,000 men in South Vietnam. Usually in support of an MEB is a single Marine Aircraft Group (MAG). The 9th MEB, however, had two MAGs in support as of March 1965. These consisted of only fixed-wing assets.

MEB Organizational Breakdown

The 9th MEB that arrived in South Vietnam in March 1965 came from the ranks of the 3d Marine Division. On paper, an MEB is usually organized to accomplish only limited missions and is typically commanded by a brigadier general. When and if that mission finishes, an MEB is reabsorbed by the next higher command level, the division.

While an MEF (Marine Expeditionary Force), the command level above a Marine division, typically oversees only a single reinforced division, it may when required manage two. The MEF is commanded by a major general or a lieutenant general, depending on its size and mission. It can be configured for different types of combat in a wide variety of geographic areas. The aviation combat element of an MEF is a Marine Aircraft Wing (MAW).

Command Structure

On 5 May 1965, Marine leadership decided in light of increasing deployment to organize all ashore as the III (3d) MEF. Two days later it would be relabelled the III Marine Amphibious Force (MAF). Its command went to two-star Major General Lewis W. Walt. By the end of 1965, the III MAF consisted of over 45,000 personnel.

Besides infantry battalions, the III MAF had by the end of 1965 eight fixed-wing squadrons, eight helicopter squadrons and a reinforced artillery regiment. In addition, it had under its control sixty-five medium tanks, twelve flame-thrower tanks, sixty-five tracked anti-tank vehicles and 157 machine-gun-armed amphibious tractors. There were also six amphibious tractors, each armed with a turret-mounted 105mm howitzer.

Marine Divisions

At the time of the Marine Corps initial large-scale commitment to the Vietnam War in 1965, the approximately 20,000-man division remained the basic building block of its combined arms ground organization. Its primary purpose was to perform amphibious assault operations as had occurred during the Second World War.

Marine divisions were also organized to execute sustained land campaigns when appropriately reinforced. Reinforcements consisted of combat support and combat service support elements. Aviation support elements were assigned depending on mission requirements, to operate from US Navy aircraft carriers until such time as air bases could be established ashore.

Reflecting the nature of the terrain and opponents faced by the Marines, division-sized ground operations were not required. Instead, infantry battalions or even companies were the key manoeuvre elements. The infantry battalions themselves were often randomly assigned to other infantry regiments for operations rather than serving under their parent infantry regimental commands.

In some cases, infantry battalions would be under the operational control or 'opcon' of a mission-specific task force headquarters. Infantry companies were also sometimes mixed and matched during operations. One Marine general reacted favourably to this practice as it '… gave the division commander great flexibility'. However, it was felt that such flexibility came at a price: 'Command lines were somewhat blurred and tactical integrity was more difficult to maintain.'

Force Troops

In 1951 the Marines dispensed with the command label of corps and substituted the name 'Force Troops'. That command organization served under the Fleet Marine Force (FMF), which corresponded to a US Army Field Army. The Force Troops of the FMF oversaw units ranging in size from regimental level to individual teams composed of only a few men. The general commanding an FMF was responsible for selecting and attaching Force Troop assets to divisions based on requirements.

Beside the combat elements of the Force Troops, such as tanks, heavy artillery and amphibious tractors, there were other equally essential units. These included a Force Service Regiment to provide Marine divisions in a combat theatre with additional logistical support. To supplement a Marine division's organic truck element, Force Troops could provide 126 trucks from a motor transport battalion.

To complement the divisional engineer elements of Marine divisions, Force Troops could contribute an engineer battalion. The engineer elements of Marine divisions tended to construct temporary works, while those of the Force Troops were responsible for projects of a more permanent nature, such as airfields, utility systems and bridges. In addition, they performed demolition services and could also operate ferries to transport men and equipment across inland waterways.

Regimental and Battalion Infantry Organization

The fighting core of Marine divisions in 1965 was their three infantry regiments, each consisting of around 3,500 men commanded by a colonel. The triangular regimental arrangement originated with the formation of the first two Marine divisions in 1940, also adopted by the US Army for its infantry divisions in the same time frame.

Early combat experience during the Vietnam War demonstrated that the Marine division's three infantry regiments provided insufficient manpower for the tasks assigned. This led to reinforcing each division with a fourth infantry regiment by 1967. Upon their departure from South Vietnam, the two Marine divisions that served in Vietnam reverted to their original three-infantry regiment structure.

Marine infantry regiments in 1965 had three infantry battalions, with approximately 1,110 men each. A division, therefore, had an authorized strength of nine infantry battalions totalling around 10,000 infantrymen. The infantry battalions also included a headquarters and service (logistical) company and a weapons company. The latter contained an 81mm mortar platoon, and an anti-tank platoon equipped with ground-mounted and wheeled vehicle-mounted 106mm recoilless rifles.

Infantry Company and Squad Organizations

Each Marine infantry battalion consisted of four infantry companies of 216 men, commanded by a headquarters section of 329 men overseen by a captain. The headquarters section directed the actions of three rifle platoons of forty-seven men each and a single weapons platoon of sixty-six men. The latter had in its inventory 3.5in rocket-launchers, eventually replaced by the Light Anti-tank Weapon (LAW), flame-throwers and 60mm mortars. A lieutenant commanded each platoon.

The rifle platoons were further divided into three rifle squads of twelve men, overseen by sergeants. The rifle squads in turn consisted of three fire teams, four-man manoeuvre elements directed by corporals. Armament for the rifle squads in 1965 consisted of the M14 rifle, the M60 machine gun and the M79 Grenade-Launcher. The M14 rifle was replaced in Marine infantry units in early 1967 by the M16 rifle and later by the improved M16A1 rifle.

Artillery Support

A critical force multiplier in the Marine divisions of 1965 was a single artillery regiment. Each Marine division artillery regiment of 2,757 men had a headquarters battery that coordinated the actions of its four artillery battalions.

Three of the four artillery battalions in a regimental artillery regiment were equipped with the towed M101A1 105mm howitzer and a single battery of the M30 107mm mortar. These formations were labelled 'direct support' battalions. The remaining artillery battalion had towed M114A1 155mm howitzers and was designated the 'general support' battalion.

In 1965, the Marines' artillery regiments in South Vietnam began replacing some of their towed 155mm howitzers with the new M109 self-propelled vehicle armed with a 155mm howitzer. However, due to the M109's size and weight, it could not be airlifted by helicopter. This left a requirement for the older 155mm towed howitzer that could be airlifted.

Typically, each of the three 105mm howitzer battalions of an artillery regiment was under the tactical control of one of the division's three infantry regiments. The single

155mm battalion (towed or self-propelled) usually remained under the tactical control of the division's artillery regiment. However, for specific operations, it too could be placed under a Marine infantry regiment's tactical control.

Area of Operation

During its time in South Vietnam, the III MAF was responsible for the security of what the US Army designated the I Corps Tactical Zone. During the Vietnam War there existed four corps tactical zones, with the II and III Zones overseen by the US Army. The IV zone was the sole responsibility of the ARVN as there were few US Army units in that area until 1967.

The I Corps Tactical Zone (hereafter referred to as I Corps) included South Vietnam's five northernmost provinces, encompassing a landmass of approximately 10,000 square miles ranging from rice paddies to steep, tropical jungle-covered mountains. I Corps' northernmost boundary was the demarcation line between North and South Vietnam, typically referred to as the 'Demilitarized Zone' (DMZ).

An estimated 2.6 million people lived within I Corps in 1965. Most lived in rural communities in the coastal regions. The other thirty-nine South Vietnamese provinces south of I Corps had an estimated population of 16.5 million people, including extensive rural areas and the large urban centre of Saigon, then the capital of South Vietnam.

The III MAF shared the responsibility of I Corps with two ARVN divisions stationed within the same area. Both the Marine and US Army units in South Vietnam were considered guests of the ARVN and did not have command authority over them; hence in theory they had to clear their plans with the local ARVN commanders before conducting any operations.

More Enclaves

On 10 April 1965, a Marine Landing Team (MLT) arrived at Phu Bai, South Vietnam, located within 7 miles of the ancient Vietnamese Imperial capital of Hue. The MLT was to establish a base for guarding the surrounding area as well as those charged with building a new military air base on site. A secondary responsibility would be protecting a nearby US Army communication unit. Phu Bai eventually became home to the headquarters of the 3d Marine Division.

In late April 1965, a high-level decision came about for the deployment of an additional 5,000 Marines from the 3d MEB, consisting of elements of the 3d Marine Division. Rather than reinforcing the troops already based around Da Nang or Phu Bai, these units were sent to set up another enclave near the South Vietnamese coastal city of Chu Lai, located 57 miles south of the Da Nang air base. Marine engineers were building another airfield that would relieve some of the overcrowding at the very busy Da Nang air base.

The 3d MEB's deployment at Chu Lai beginning on 7 May and running through to 12 May 1965 was unopposed. The engineers had the air base up and running by 1 June 1965. Chu Lai eventually became home to the headquarters of the 1st Marine Division.

With the 3d MEB's arrival, the bulk of the 3d Marine Division was in place. It was at this point in June of 1965 that both the 3d and 9th MEBs were deactivated and reverted to their parent command, the 3d Marine Division.

In June 1965, a single Marine rifle battalion was assigned to form another protective enclave around a US Army logistical base and airfield at the coastal city of Qui Nho'n. The city lay 188 miles south of the Da Nang air base.

Early Offensive Activities

The role of the 9th MEB at the Da Nang air base remained strictly defensive until 1 April 1965, when President Johnson authorized them to go on limited offensive patrols. The first began on 20 April 1965. Two days later a small patrol composed of Marines and an AVRN unit encountered an enemy force, with one Viet Cong (VC) killed and a single Marine wounded in the ensuing engagement.

There would be other battles between the VC and the Marines between March and June 1965. In these fights the Marines lost 34 killed and 134 wounded. VC losses were 270 killed. With enough troops and equipment in place and with the formation of the III MAF, the Marine leadership was approved to mount larger offensive operations beginning in July 1965.

In July 1965, the III MAF commander in a written directive to his men stressed '… the indiscriminate or unnecessary use of weapons is counterproductive. The injury

---

Enemy Terms

A literal translation of 'Viet Cong' is 'Vietnamese Communist'. The official name of the Viet Cong, or VC for short, was the National Front for the Liberation of South Vietnam (NFLSVN). Despite trying to portray itself as an ingenuous South Vietnamese-led force, it was always directed by the North Vietnamese communist leadership of the Democratic Republic of Vietnam (DRV). The DRV's military arm was the People's Army of Vietnam (PAVN), or the North Vietnamese Army (NVA).

From a US military pamphlet comes a description of the two types of VC personnel encountered by American military forces: 'The Viet Cong's full military element also is divided into two types: the Regional Forces and the Main Force … The elite units of the so-called Liberation Army are the battalions of the Main Forces.' They typically did not have the most modern weapons and equipment employed by the NVA.

or killing of hapless civilians inevitably contributes to the Communist cause, and each incident of it will be used against us with telling effect.'

The Enemy Strikes Back

In spite of more offensively-orientated Marine patrols, the VC mounted a successful hit-and-run attack on the massive Da Nang air base at midnight on 1 July 1965. It consisted of an eighty-five-man enemy unit armed with mortars, machine guns and demolition charges. Destroying three aircraft and damaging two more, they escaped with only one casualty, a member captured by an ARVN unit.

On the evenings of 27 and 28 October 1965, the enemy successfully attacked two Marine airfields: a helicopter facility located on the Tien Sha Peninsula and the Chu Lai air base. Colonel Leslie E. Brown, who was at Chu Lai when it was attacked, remembered the first thing that he and the other Marines present knew of the enemy attack: the sound of machine-gun fire and demolition charges going off. He would recall:

> ... a couple of the airplanes were on fire, and the sappers [demolition experts] had gotten through intact ... they were barefooted and had on a loincloth, and it was kind of a John Wayne dramatic effect. They had Thompson submachine guns, and they were spraying the airplanes with the Tommy guns and ... throwing satchel charges into [aircraft] tailpipes ... Some went off and some didn't, but the net effect was that the machine-gun fire caused leaks in the fuel tanks, so the JP fuel was drenching the whole area...and in the middle of that, the airplanes were on fire.

Of the twenty VC who attacked the Chu Lai air base, the Marines killed fifteen for the loss of two planes destroyed and severe damage to six more. The enemy attack on the Marine helicopter base on the Tien Sha Peninsula consisted of ninety men divided into four separate demolition teams. Under cover of mortar fire, they managed to destroy nineteen helicopters and damage another thirty-five, as well as damage a new hospital under construction. The attackers lost seventeen dead and four wounded. The Marines had three killed and ninety-one wounded.

From the Marine Corps Historical Branch monograph titled *Marines and Helicopters 1962–1963* by Lieutenant Colonel William R. Fails comes the following passage on the enemy attack on the Marine Tien Sha Peninsula helicopter base:

> Three and possibly four teams conducted the assault. One unit attempted to breach the defenses near the H&MS [Headquarters and Maintenance Squadron] hangar. There they met Mortimer, O'Shannon and Brule. 'We'd been in the hole only about 20 seconds when we saw about eight people, all armed, running towards us,' said O'Shannon. 'They were about 30 to 40 feet away. We

saw they were Viet Cong. When they got within 15 feet of us, we opened fire with our rifles.' Their Marine Corps training paid off well. All three happened to be 'expert' riflemen and annihilated the enemy squad, killing seven and wounding and capturing four others.

Additional Enemy Attacks

A planned enemy attack on the air base at Da Nang, to have been conducted on the evening of 28 October, might have been foiled by a couple of occurrences. First, the III MAF received information the day before of an approaching VC main force battalion 10 miles south of the air base. In response, an artillery barrage was directed into the area they were thought to be. By default, this alerted the enemy to the fact that a surprise attack on the Da Nang air base would now be out of the question.

A Marine infantry squad ambushed a strong VC main force 5 miles south of the Da Nang air base on the night of 28 October. Realizing that they were significantly outnumbered, the Marines withdrew under a protective screen of 81mm mortar fire. Before retiring, they counted fifteen dead enemy soldiers in front of their position as the enemy forces disengaged from the ambush.

On 30 October 1965, the VC attempted to capture a company-sized Marine Corps defensive position labelled Hill 22. It lay south of Da Nang air base next to the Tuy Loan River. The attack began when ten to fifteen enemy soldiers walked into a Marine ambush. Despite losing the element of surprise, the VC pressed the attack two hours later in much larger numbers and managed to capture a portion of the Marine position before being driven off. They suffered forty-seven dead and one wounded. Marine casualties were sixteen killed and forty-one wounded.

The First Big Battle

In early August 1965, the III MAF became aware of an approximately 1,500-man VC main force regiment located on the Phuoc Thuan Peninsula. The enemy-occupied peninsula lay just 12 miles south of the Marine enclave of Chu Lai, the anticipated goal of the enemy regiment.

Rather than wait for the enemy to attack first, the III MAF quickly arranged for a two-infantry battalion force to deploy near the VC-occupied area beginning on 17 August. The Marines came by sea and air in what became known as Operation STARLITE.

Initially, the Marines faced minimal resistance and losses as they advanced towards the expected location of the enemy regiment on 18 August. That soon changed, and they encountered strong opposition from the combat-experienced VC regiment. One airlifted Marine rifle company was unknowingly deposited directly on top of an emplaced VC battalion, leading to fierce fighting and damage to numerous Marine helicopters.

The fierceness of the fighting on 18 August appears in the awarding of Medals of Honor to two Marines fighting in Operation STARLITE. Corporal Robert Emmett O'Malley earned one of these when his squad came under heavy fire from a dug-in enemy unit. Rather than seek cover, according to his Medal of Honor citation, he: '... raced across an open rice paddy to a trench line where the enemy forces were located. Jumping into the trench, he attacked the Viet Cong with his rifle and grenades, and singly killed 8 of the enemy.'

O'Malley's daring exploits continued throughout the remainder of the 18 August engagement. From his citation: 'Although three times wounded in the encounter, and facing imminent death from a fanatic and determined enemy, he steadfastly refused evacuation and continued to cover his squad's boarding of the helicopters while, from an exposed position, he delivered fire against the enemy until his wounded men were evacuated.'

Fire Support

Other Marine ground units began encountering stiff enemy resistance on 18 August, despite strong support from F-4 Phantoms and A-4 Skyhawks of five different Marine squadrons. The squadrons flew seventy-eight sorties (missions) on 18 August and in the process dropped 65 tons of bombs, 4 tons of napalm and fired hundreds of 2.75in rockets and thousands of rounds of 20mm ammunition.

Then Colonel Leslie E. Brown, a Marine officer during Operation STARLITE, stated in a 14 August 1975 interview conducted by the Marine Historical Center:

> The Marines were in trouble ... and our airplanes were literally just staying in the flight pattern, and they'd land and re-arm and take off, be right back again in a few minutes just dropping and strafing and firing rockets ... in the three-day period, we flew more sorties than in the history of any other attack group before or since in support of that one operation which took place ... in an area probably about 2 miles square.

In addition to aerial support, the Marines on the ground had both Marine artillery support as well as fire support from three US Navy warships. On 19 August a group of around 100 enemy personnel was observed on a beach by a US Navy destroyer in what appeared to be an attempt to escape. They found themselves engaged by the destroyer's 5in guns, which caused them severe losses. The ship also sank seven sampans that the enemy had obtained as part of their aborted escape attempt.

The Ending of STARLITE

Owing to the immense firepower advantage enjoyed by the Marines, including tanks, the remaining elements of the VC regiment trapped on the Phuoc Thuan Peninsula slipped through the Marine cordon on the night of 18 August. There remained left behind enemy elements that had to be subdued, one by one, extending Operation STARLITE through to 24 August.

At the conclusion of Operation STARLITE, the Marines counted 614 enemy soldiers killed on the battlefield, with 9 taken prisoner and another 42 enemy suspects taken into custody. Marine losses were 45 dead and 203 wounded. A Marine regimental commander involved in Operation STARLITE had this to say about the tanks they had in support: 'The tanks were certainly the difference between extremely heavy casualties and the number we actually took. Every place the tanks went, they drew a crowd of VC.'

The Marines were proud of the outcome of their first major battle with the enemy. However, they also learned that VC main force units were a formidable foe and had to be respected. ARVN generals were not impressed with the destruction of the VC main force regiment, as they had seen VC units quickly re-formed and on the battlefield months later.

In Pursuit of the Enemy

To finish off the enemy regiment engaged during Operation STARLITE, the III MAF mounted a number of operations in cooperation with ARVN forces from September through to November 1965 without much success, as the VC regiment refused to enter into combat with them. In early November 1965, the VC commenced attacks against the weaker ARVN forces.

Despite Marine aerial support and ARVN replacements, on the morning of 10 December the VC regiment attacked once again and overran one of the ARVN regiment's two battalions. At this point, on 10 December, the III MAF committed two Marine infantry battalions to the fight.

Once engaged in the battle, the Marines also suffered substantial casualties at the hands of the VC regiment. Additional Marines were therefore committed to the fight on 11 December, but the enemy had already disengaged from the battle and successfully withdrew.

The Marines decided to track down the VC regiment and engage it in battle, which they managed to do on 18 December at a location known as Ky Phu. Confronted by Marine artillery fire and aerial support, the enemy quickly realized that the odds were against them and attempted to withdraw. First Lieutenant Nicholas H. Grosz, who had accompanied one of the Marine infantry companies on the operation, stated: 'Once we got them going, the VC just broke and ran. It was just like a turkey shoot.'

By the time the engagement between the Marines and the enemy regiment concluded on 20 December, the Marine and ARVN combined operation had claimed 407 enemy troops killed and thirty-three captured, with many weapons and supplies seized. Marine losses came to forty-five killed and ninety wounded. ARVN losses were reported as ninety killed, ninety-one missing and 141 wounded.

The Helicopter Role

A significant contributing factor to the Marine success during its initial battles with the main force VC lay with the support from various Marine helicopter units. Flying more than 9,230 sorties, these units carried approximately 12,117 troops and transported over 600 tons of supplies. Marine UH-1E helicopter gunships, armed with machine guns and rockets, provided close air support when Marine jets could not carry out their missions due to poor visibility.

Besides moving infantry around the battlefield, Marine helicopters also performed many other vital roles including reconnaissance and medical evacuation. The enemy attempted to shoot down Marine helicopters on more than a hundred occasions during the operation. A total of fifty-three helicopters were damaged, but only two destroyed. Personnel losses among the helicopter crews proved to be only one killed and twelve wounded.

The 1965 Summary

During the last half of 1965, the III MAF had conducted fifteen operations consisting of battalions or larger units. Essential lessons on what had and hadn't worked came out of these various operations. However, despite these numerous operations, on 10 December 1965 General Westmoreland stressed in a letter to all his subordinate commanders that more aggressive operations were required on their part against main force VC formations for the US forces in Vietnam to stand a chance of success. The commander of the III MAF had anticipated this development, and had in the summer of 1965 informed his superiors that more Marines would be required.

Former Vice President Lyndon B. Johnson, seen here, took presidential office following the assassination of President John F. Kennedy on 22 November 1963. Johnson entered into office having to deal with the faltering government of South Vietnam and its military. He was, however, convinced that with American military assistance the South Vietnamese could prevail over the Viet Cong. (*DOD*)

(**Opposite, above**) The first Marine Corps formation to arrive in South Vietnam in 1965 was a Light Anti-Aircraft Missile (LAAM) Battalion on 8 February. The unit's armament consisted of the Hawk anti-aircraft missile system pictured here on its launching unit. The radar-guided missile had an effective slant range of 15 miles and a maximum effective ceiling of 65,000ft. (*USMC*)

(**Opposite, below**) The Hawk was 12ft 6in in length, with a diameter of 14in and a wingspan of about 4ft. It weighed 1,295lb and contained a 120lb warhead with contact and radio-based proximity fuses. In support of the LAAM Battalion, a company of Marine engineers landed by sea near Da Nang air base on 17 February 1965. (*USMC*)

(**Above**) On 8 March 1965, elements of the 9th Marine Expeditionary Brigade (MEB) landed near the Da Nang air base. Included among the equipment they brought were the M48A3 medium tanks seen here on board a US Navy landing craft. The diesel-engine-powered A3 version of the M48 series had entered Marine Corps service in late 1964. (*USMC*)

(**Opposite, above**) Elements of the 9th MEB were also airlifted into Da Nang air base from Okinawa on 8 March 1965, in US Air Force (USAF) transport aircraft. Unlike those elements of the 9th MEB that had come by sea, those that came by aircraft were subjected to sporadic ground fire that fortunately scored no hits. (*USMC*)

(**Above**) The Marines of the 9th MEB were not the first deployed to South Vietnam. A Marine Helicopter Transport Squadron Light HMR(L) had previously been deployed in South Vietnam in April 1962 to aid the Army of the Republic of Vietnam (ARVN). They flew the Sikorsky UH-34 pictured here. Originally designated the 'HUS-1', the UH-34 had entered Marine Corps service in 1957. (*USMC*)

(**Opposite, below**) Prior to the Marine Helicopter Transport Squadron Light HMR(L)'s arrival in South Vietnam in 1962, Marine Corps advisers had been in the country since 1954. Pictured here is one of the advisers pointing out the various features of a Browning Automatic Rifle (BAR) to a South Vietnamese Marine. Besides advising the South Vietnamese Marine Corps, the US Marine advisers did the same for some ARVN units. (*USMC*)

On arriving in South Vietnam, the men of the 9th MEB found themselves restricted to only being observers. The American Joint Chiefs of Staff (JCS) forbade them in a 7 March 1965 directive that stated: 'US Marine Force will not, repeat, will not, engage in day-to-day actions against the Viet Cong.' Guarding the Da Nang air base remained the responsibility of the ARVN. (*USMC*)

Marines are shown here coming ashore in South Vietnam. Before the arrival of the 9th MEB there were on 28 February 1965 a total of 1,248 Marines in and around the Da Nang air base. These included a security company of 260 men assigned to guard the Marine Helicopter Transport Squadron Light HMR(L) based at Da Nang. (*USMC*)

By 23 March 1965, with the arrival of the 9th MEB, there were 4,612 men in and around the Da Nang air base. Of that number, 583 belonged to a Brigade Logistic Support Group. Unfortunately, the Marine logistic system intended to support the 9th MEB quickly broke down, resulting in serious shortages of everything from rations to artillery ammunition. (*USMC*)

As there was no suitable highway infrastructure in South Vietnam to handle the amount of truck traffic required to support Marine units, heavy engineering equipment such as the compactor pictured here was employed in building roads from dawn to dusk, seven days a week. Mechanics had to work every night to have the equipment ready for the next day. (*USMC*)

(**Opposite, above**) It would not be for lack of trying that the Marine logistical system in South Vietnam failed early on. The Marine Corps had a then state-of-the-art computerized supply system. However, once in the country, the computer stock cards (punch cards), according to a report, 'began swelling due to the high humidity and the cards wouldn't fit in the machine [computer].' Everything, therefore, had to be done manually. (*USMC*)

(**Opposite, below**) Adding to the Marine Corps' logistical support problems was the lack of adequate unloading facilities at the port of Da Nang, causing supply ships to remain in Da Nang harbour for two weeks or longer before having a chance to unload their cargos. Pictured here are cargo ships docked at the port of Da Nang. (*US Navy*)

(**Opposite, above**) Pictured here is a Marine armed with an M14 rifle in South Vietnam. The M14 had a twenty-round box magazine that inserted into the bottom of its receiver. As of 20 April 1965, the 9th MEB in South Vietnam consisted of 8,607 men with the majority stationed around the Da Nang air base. On that same day, they gained permission to engage in aggressive patrolling. (*USMC*)

(**Opposite, below**) On 22 April 1965, the Marines of the 9th MEB had their first encounter with the Viet Cong, losing one man and claiming one enemy soldier killed. On 29 April 1965, the Marines participated in their first combined operation with the ARVN. Searching a village for any signs of the Viet Cong, such as weapons or ammo, is a Marine in the foreground with an M14 rifle and an ARVN soldier equipped with an M1 Garand. (*USMC*)

(**Above**) The M14 rifle seen here in the hands of a Marine in South Vietnam proved somewhat unsuitable in theatre for a variety of reasons. These included its inability to be fired accurately in fully-automatic mode, reliability issues and parts breaking. Its weight and size also caused issues in the often close confines of the country's terrain. (*USMC*)

On 20 April 1965, President Johnson committed a Marine Expeditionary Force (MEF) to Da Nang. The initial elements of the III MEF arrived at Da Nang on 3 May 1965. Pictured here are Marine engineers constructing steel matting for a boat ramp. On 7 May 1965, the III MEF became the Marine Amphibious Force (MAF). *(USMC)*

As of 30 May 1965, there were approximately 17,000 Marines in South Vietnam, with the largest number (9,224) operating out of the Da Nang air base. Another 6,599 were at Chu Lai. On 4 June 1965, three-star Major General Lewis W. Walt took command of the III MEF, which included all Marine Corps personnel within I Corps. In this post-Vietnam War photograph, we see him as a four-star general. (*USMC*)

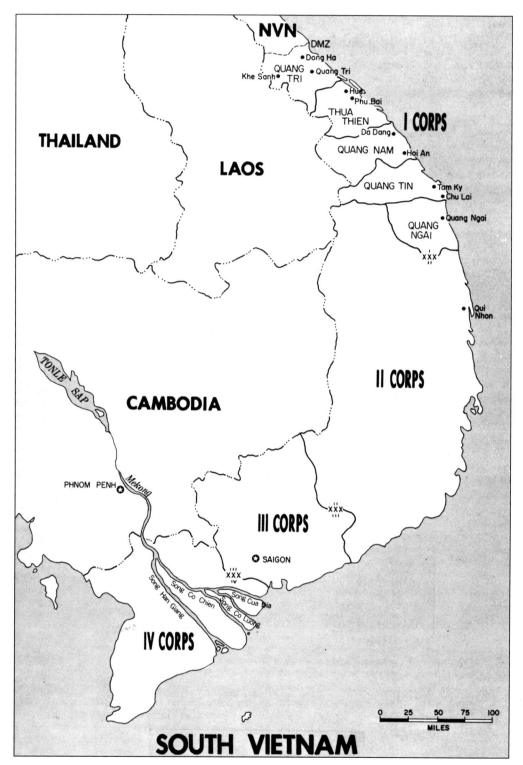

Founded in October 1955, South Vietnam consisted of forty-four provinces of varying size and population. Militarily it was divided into four corps zones numbered one to four (as seen in this map). The III MAF was assigned the security of the five northernmost provinces of the country, which fell within the I Corps' region of responsibility. (*USMC*)

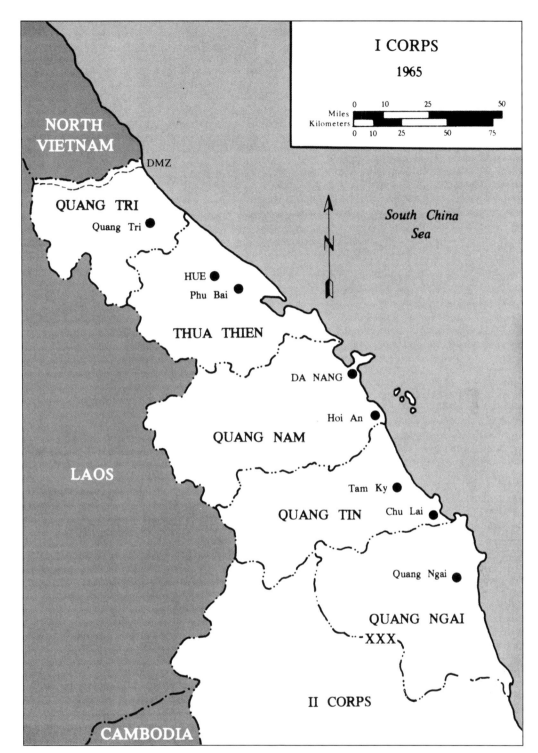

In this map of the five northernmost provinces, the III MAF's zone of responsibility, lay Da Nang, the home of the largest and most important Marine Corps base in the country from 1965 until 1971. The border that divided North Vietnam and South Vietnam was referred to as the Demilitarized Zone (DMZ) by the American military and also appears on the map. (*USMC*)

(**Opposite, above**) The III MAF had as its organic air support the 1st Marine Aircraft Wing (MAW). The 1st MAW had a personnel strength of approximately 13,000 men and was subdivided into Marine Aircraft Groups (MAGs), including both fixed-wing and helicopter squadrons. Pictured here is a Marine A-4 Skyhawk, a single-seat light-attack bomber. (*USMC*)

(**Opposite, below**) The primary purpose of the fixed-wing MAGs was the support of Marine Corps ground formations. They also provided armed escorts to Marine helicopter formations. Pictured here is an F-8 Crusader, a type that first entered into Marine Corps' service in 1956. Originally intended as an interceptor, it saw useful service as a close-support aircraft during the Vietnam War. (*USMC*)

(**Above**) The biggest issue facing the 1st MAW was who would oversee its actions. The Marines felt that the USAF had not effectively employed Marine air assets during the Korean War (1950–53) and did not want to repeat that arrangement in Vietnam. The Marine Corps' leadership, however, was overruled and certain fixed-wing Marine squadrons fell under USAF command beginning in 1965. Shown here is an F-8 Crusader. (*USMC*)

Ground crewmen are loading 20mm ammunition into a Marine F-8 Crusader. Another type of mission performed by the 1st MAW bore the name 'direct air support'. In this case, aircraft would not operate in support of ground formation. Rather, they performed missions directed at isolating the enemy from the battlefield and destroying their support bases. (*USMC*)

(**Opposite, above**) Two basic types of 'close air support' missions took place during the Vietnam War. One received the name 'pre-planned'. Requests for such had to be placed twenty hours ahead by ground commanders. That request would pass to the Direct Air Support Center (DASC) and the Tactical Air Direction Center (TADC) for approval and coordination. Pictured here during a close-support mission is an F-8 Crusader. (*USMC*)

(**Opposite, below**) Another type of close air support mission flown by the 1st MAW during the Vietnam War bore the name 'on-call'. Its title is self-explanatory and could be made in emergencies by aircraft already in the air intended for such missions, or by diverting aircraft from other missions. The F-4 Phantom II pictured here was the eventual replacement for the F-8 Crusader in South Vietnam. (*USMC*)

(**Above**) To avoid friendly-fire incidents by Marine fixed-wing aircraft supporting ground formations, Marine tactical air coordinators (TACs) provided oversight. Several modified aircraft types were employed by the TACs. One such was the two-seat TF-9J Cougar trainer aircraft pictured here. Other TAC platforms included a light propeller-driven aircraft or a helicopter gunship. (*USMC*)

(**Opposite, above**) The 1967 replacement for the two-seat TF-9J Cougar in the TAC role would be the two-seat trainer TA-4F Skyhawk shown here. Like its predecessor, the TA-4F Skyhawk had wing-mounted rocket pods for marking targets for the weapon-carrying jet aircraft. The TACs maintained contact with ground units via FM radios while directing attack aircraft with UAF radios. (*USMC*)

(**Opposite, below**) On occasion, the fixed-wing ground-based squadrons of the 1st MAW also crossed into North Vietnam to suppress enemy anti-aircraft defences during rescue missions for the pilots and air-crew of downed USAF aircraft. Other Marine fixed-wing squadrons flying off aircraft carriers flew attack missions all over South Vietnam and North Vietnam. Pictured here is a Marine F-4 Phantom II. (*USMC*)

(**Opposite, above**) When venturing over North Vietnam, the fixed-wing jet aircraft of the 1st MAW found themselves subjected to a wide range of Soviet-designed anti-aircraft guns. One of these, seen here, was the S-60, a towed short-to-medium-range single-barrel 57mm anti-aircraft gun. Besides an on-carriage optical fire-control system, it could also be controlled by an off-carriage radar-directed fire-control system. (*Vladimir Yakubov*)

(**Above**) The most important military sites in North Vietnam were protected by the Soviet-designed and built radar-guided SA-2 Guideline anti-aircraft missile system pictured here. Introduced into Soviet Army service in 1959, it would be supplied to the North Vietnamese military beginning in 1965. The missile had a slant range of up to 31 miles and a maximum altitude of 82,000ft. (*Vladimir Yakubov*)

(**Opposite, below**) To protect Marine aircraft (as well as other friendly planes) over North Vietnam and Laos, there would be the EF-10B Skynight pictured here that served until 1969 as electronic warfare (EW) aircraft. It identified enemy radar systems in the electronic intelligence (ELINT) role and then jammed them in the electronic countermeasure (ECM) role. (*USMC*)

(**Opposite, above**) Photo reconnaissance missions over both South and North Vietnam as well as Laos were performed by the RF-8A pictured here, employed by both the US Navy and Marine Corps. The RF-8A was a version of the F-8 Crusader series. Besides identifying possible enemy targets, it would return once a target was struck to verify the results. (*US Navy*)

(**Opposite, below**) Marine UH-34 helicopters are shown here refuelling on a South Vietnamese beach. In theory, the UH-34 was taken into service by the Marine Corps in 1957 only as a utility (jack-of-all-trades) helicopter. However, when procurement of a larger dedicated assault troop transport helicopter failed to materialize, the UH-34 filled in as a stop-gap assault troop transport in South Vietnam until 1969. (*USMC*)

(**Above**) The M14 rifle-equipped Marines in the foreground are seen here lining up for transport by the UH-34 helicopters in the background. The helicopter had the unofficial nickname of the 'Dog', based on the last letter of its designation. Another popular unofficial nickname for the helicopter was 'HUS', based on its original pre-1962 designation as the HUS-1. (*USMC*)

The troop compartment of the UH-34 as pictured here was placed directly under the main transmission and rotor, with the pilots and engine in front, counterbalanced by a long tail structure in the rear. The cabin measured over 13ft long, almost 5ft wide and was 6ft high with a large sliding door on the right side. There were canvas bucket seats for twelve passengers. *(USMC)*

The Marine Corps UH-34s and all the other helicopters of its time were both unarmoured and slow, making them extremely vulnerable to enemy ground fire, especially when approaching or departing from landing zones. One of the most dangerous threats came from the Soviet-designed, optically-guided tripod-mounted DShKM 1938/46 machine gun pictured here that fired a 12.7mm round.
(USAF Museum)

DShK-1938/46 Heavy Ma

A Deadly "Sweetie"

Used by communist forces in Southeast Asia, the Degtyarev-Shpagin Krupnokaliberny (DShK) machine gun presented a deadly threat to low flying aircraft, like the Forward Air Controllers (FACs). Sometimes called Dushka (meaning "Sweetie"), they could be mounted on armored vehicles or tripods as anti-aircraft (AA) weapons. To avoid these weapons, aircraft had to fly higher, making them vulnerable to heavy-caliber anti-aircraft artillery (AAA) and surface to air missiles (SAM).

This DShK-1938/46, an improved version of the DShK-1938 used by Soviet forces in World War II, incorporated a more reliable feeding mechanism for its 12.7mm x 108mm ammunition (Krupnokaliberny translates as "large caliber") which was roughly equivalent to the American .50 caliber. From the 1940s on, the DShK was manufactured by many communist nations and still remains in use today around the world.

42

Visible in this photograph from the interior of a Marine Corps UH-34 helicopter in South Vietnam is the side door gunner armed with an M60 machine gun. Before the fitting of the M60, the UH-34s in the theatre had Second World War-era Browning M1919A4 air-cooled .30 calibre machine guns. (*USMC*)

(**Above**) The optically-guided ZPU-23-2 shown here had two automatic 23mm cannons. Introduced into Soviet Army service in 1960, it had a practical rate of fire of 400 rounds per minute. The ZPU-23-2 would be supplied to the North Vietnamese Army in large numbers and, firing a high-explosive (HE) round, took a heavy toll of American military helicopters during the Vietnam War. (*Vladimir Yakubov*)

(**Opposite, above**) A Soviet-designed anti-aircraft gun supplied to the North Vietnamese Army in large numbers would be the optically-guided M1939 (61-K) anti-aircraft gun pictured here. Armed with a 37mm automatic cannon, it had a rate of fire between 160-170 rounds per minute. It had a maximum effective range of approximately 3 miles and an effective ceiling of 16,000ft. (*Vladimir Yakubov*)

(**Opposite, below**) In this illustration, we see the theoretical table of organization and equipment (TO&E) for the 3d Marine Division when it achieved full strength in South Vietnam at the end of 1965. Of the approximately 20,000 men in the division, its core fighting strength consisted of its three infantry regiments totalling 7,500 men. Supporting fire for the infantry regiments came from a single artillery regiment of around 2,800 men. (*USMC*)

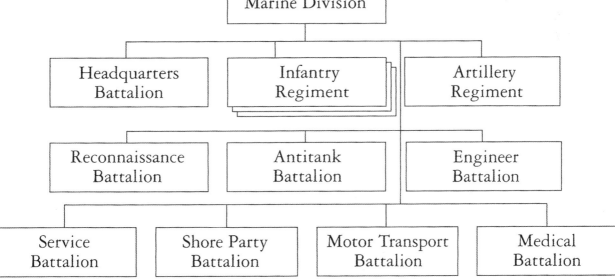

```
                         ┌─────────────────┐
                         │ Marine Division │
                         └─────────────────┘

┌──────────────┐      ┌──────────────┐      ┌──────────────┐
│ Headquarters │      │  Infantry    │      │  Artillery   │
│  Battalion   │      │  Regiment    │      │  Regiment    │
└──────────────┘      └──────────────┘      └──────────────┘

┌────────────────┐    ┌──────────────┐      ┌──────────────┐
│ Reconnaissance │    │  Antitank    │      │  Engineer    │
│   Battalion    │    │  Battalion   │      │  Battalion   │
└────────────────┘    └──────────────┘      └──────────────┘

┌──────────────┐  ┌──────────────┐  ┌───────────────────┐  ┌──────────────┐
│   Service    │  │ Shore Party  │  │  Motor Transport  │  │   Medical    │
│  Battalion   │  │  Battalion   │  │     Battalion     │  │  Battalion   │
└──────────────┘  └──────────────┘  └───────────────────┘  └──────────────┘
```

The headquarters battalion for a Marine division oversaw a scout-sniper platoon broken down into two-person teams. One was armed with a dedicated long-range sniper rifle as seen in this photograph, and his spotter with a standard infantry rifle. Reflecting their label, the primary role of the scout-sniper teams was reconnaissance and surveillance in support of Marine infantry battalions. (USMC)

Each of the three infantry regiments of a Marine division in 1965 was subdivided into three infantry battalions of 1,193 men. The individual infantry battalion was directed by a headquarters and service company of 329 men. Marine infantry battalions had little organic transport and, if not provided with attached vehicles or helicopters, walked everywhere. (USMC)

Each Marine infantry battalion had four infantry companies with a combined total of 864 men, each overseen by a nine-man headquarters section. In theory, infantry companies were to be commanded by captains but were often commanded by lieutenants due to casualties. The belted rounds carried by the Marine pictured here were for an M60 machine gun. (*USMC*)

(**Opposite, above**) Each Marine infantry company of 216 men was further subdivided into three infantry platoons of forty-seven men each and a single weapons platoon of sixty-six men. The three rifle platoons were each sub-divided into three squad fire teams composed of four men each. Of those four men, one would be assigned as the fire team leader and normally held the rank of corporal. (*USMC*)

(**Opposite, below**) Eventually, Marine squads received the M79 Grenade-Launcher pictured here. The single-shot weapon could fire a 40mm high-explosive (HE) grenade out to a maximum range of 427 yards. It could also fire other munitions, including a smoke round. It had unofficial nicknames including 'Bloop Gun' and 'Thumper' for the sound it made when fired. (*USMC*)

(**Above**) In each M14 rifle-equipped Marine fire team, one of the four men bore the title 'automatic rifleman'. He had a modified version of the M14 rifle optimized for fully-automatic fire, designated the M14A1. The main source of firepower for Marine platoons would be the M60 machine guns, as shown here, that belonged to the infantry company's weapons platoon. (*USMC*)

The mortar section of the weapons platoon in Marine rifle companies had a non-commissioned officer (NCO) that oversaw three 60mm mortar squads. Each mortar squad of five men operated a single 60mm M19 Mortar as shown here. The M19 had a sustained rate of fire of approximately eighteen rounds per minute and a maximum range of just under 2,000 yards. (*USMC*)

(**Opposite, above**) The larger 81mm Mortar M29 pictured here appeared at the Marine infantry battalion levels in the battalion headquarters and service company. It had entered into service in the early 1960s with an improved version labelled the M29A1. With a sustained rate of fire of eighteen rounds per minute, it had a maximum range of approximately 3 miles. (*USMC*)

(**Opposite, below**) Also located in the battalion headquarters and service company of Marine infantry battalions was a small assault section. It had a few of the 3.5in M20 Rocket-Launchers as seen here. Better known by its popular nickname of the 'Bazooka', the M20 did not appear in American military service until after the Second World War, but did see service with the Marine Corps during the Korean War. (*USMC*)

(**Opposite, above**) The eventual Vietnam War replacement for the Marines' 3.5in M20 Rocket-Launcher proved to be the M72 Light Anti-tank Weapon (LAW) pictured here. It was a self-contained one-shot, disposable, shaped-charge anti-tank rocket-launcher. Weighing 2lb, it had a maximum effective range of 328 yards at point targets. (*USMC*)

(**Above**) The Marine Corps had made very successful use of its man-portable flame-throwers during the Second World War and continued to value them post-war. By the time of the Vietnam War, the version employed would be designated the M9A1-7 seen here in use. Often used in terrain clearance, it also remained effective against enemy bunkers during the conflict. (*USMC*)

(**Opposite, below**) The most powerful anti-tank weapon found in the 1965 Marine Division TO&E was the M40 106mm Recoilless Rifle pictured here that appeared in service with the Marine Corps after the Korean War. It weighed 461lb on a tripod and fired a 37lb shaped-charge, high-explosive (HE) anti-tank warhead with a maximum effective range of about 8,000 yards. (*USMC*)

(**Opposite, above**) Due to the weight of the M40 106mm Recoilless Rifle, the Marine Corps had a couple of vehicles that could carry it into action. These included the vehicle pictured here which had a couple of official designations including the M274 Truck Platform Utility 0.5-ton 4 x 4. To many it was known by various unofficial nicknames, such as the 'Mule' or the 'Mechanical Mule'. (*USMC*)

(**Above**) The very ungainly-looking vehicle shown here in Marine Corps' service during the Vietnam War was the Multiple 106mm Self-Propelled Rifle M50A1 and officially nicknamed the 'Ontos' (Greek: the 'thing'). Allis-Chalmers built 360 examples of the vehicle for the Marine Corps with the first production unit delivered on 31 October 1956. (*USMC*)

(**Opposite, below**) The six recoilless rifles of the Multiple 106mm Self-Propelled Rifle M50A1 were attached to a small pivoting fixture on the very top of the three-person hull that allowed the weapons to be elevated and traversed. The weapons had a maximum traverse of 40 degrees to either side of the vehicle's centreline and a maximum elevation of 20 degrees. (*USMC*)

(**Above**) The single artillery regiment in the TO&E of the 1965 Marine division had four different weapons. The most numerous, pictured here, was the towed 105mm Howitzer M101A1 that had entered service with the Marine Corps during the Second World War. The weapon's maximum rate of fire was ten rounds per minute for the first three minutes, with a sustained rate of fire of three to five rounds per minute. (*USMC*)

(**Opposite**) Dating from the Second World War but seeing service during the Vietnam War in a Marine division's artillery regiment would be the 4.2in (107mm Mortar) M30 shown here. The weapon, unofficially nicknamed the 'four-deuce', fired a 27lb HE round to an approximate range of 3 miles. It normally took an eight-man team to service the weapon. (*USMC*)

(**Opposite**) Due to its 650lb weight when in firing order, the 4.2in (107mm Mortar) M30 could only be moved short distances by its crew. To overcome this drawback, the Marine Corps came up with a makeshift arrangement of mounting the weapon on the towed gun carriage of the obsolete 75mm M1 Pack Howitzer. The resulting weapon received the designation M98 and the unofficial nickname of the 'Howtar'. (*USMC*)

(**Above**) The largest towed artillery piece in a 1965 Marine division would be the M114A1 155mm howitzer pictured here. Like the 105mm Howitzer M101A1, the weapon's design dated from the Second World War. It had a maximum effective range of about 9 miles with a 95lb HE round. Unlike the M101A1 which was classified as a light artillery piece, the M114A1 received the classification of a medium artillery piece. (*USMC*)

Chapter Two

The Fighting Increases in Scope (1966–67)

In 1966, the III MAF gained the 1st Marine Division, although elements of the division had been in South Vietnam since July 1965. The bulk of the division arrived in-country between January and June 1966 and was stood up in July 1966. The III MAF assigned it responsibility for the security of the three southernmost provinces of I Corps in October 1966.

At the same time that the 1st Division took over the responsibility of the three southernmost provinces of I Corps, the 3d Marine Division took on sole responsibility for the two northernmost provinces of I Corps. Elements of the 5th Marine Division were also deployed to South Vietnam to reinforce both the 1st and 3d Marine divisions. By the end of 1966, the III MAF had 66,000 men.

The US Army Dictates

As the numbers of Marines in I Corps grew, in 1966 the Military Assistance Command, Vietnam (MACV), overseen by US Army four-star general William C. Westmoreland, wanted the majority of III MAF's assets immediately devoted to conducting large-scale 'search-and-destroy' operations. These were intended to take place in the relatively unpopulated mountainous and jungle-covered hinterlands of I Corps' five provinces where the enemy supposedly resided.

Westmoreland believed throughout his command during the Vietnam War that if enough of the enemy were killed, the rest would be forced to concede. Search and destroy became the standard operating practice of US Army divisions based in the II and III Corps areas under his direct control. He turned over pacification programmes to the South Vietnamese government and military, even after stating that they were not up to the task.

The Marine Viewpoint

Senior Marine commanders felt from the beginning of 1966 that their resources would be better devoted to initially conducting small-scale unit security and pacification programmes. These were to take place along the densely-populated coastal regions of I Corps. The intended goal was to eliminate the VC cadre that lived among the rural communities and encourage inhabitants to support the South Vietnamese government.

In a US military pamphlet appears this description of the cadre and their role in a typical South Vietnamese village: '… trained, dedicated, hard-core Communist leaders and military officers … a cadre's role can best be described as a combination priest, policeman, and propagandist'.

Colonel George W. Carrington, Jr, the 3d Marine Division G-2 (intelligence officer), wrote in January 1966 regarding the importance of security and pacification programmes:

> … to reassure the villagers that they were safe, supported and protected, US Marines undertook a most demanding pattern of intensive, multiple, day-and-night, tedious patrol activity. The incredible total of man-hours devoted to this end and the sincere, compassionate, and dedicated manner in which thousands of Marines did their duty were never understood or appreciated by outsiders.

Arguing the Point

Marine Lieutenant General Victor H. Krulak, a specialist in counter-insurgency and the commander of the Fleet Marine Force/Pacific (FMF/Pac), the command level above the III MAF, stated his opinion on the importance of security and pacification programmes: 'There was no virtue at all in seeking out the enemy in the mountains and jungles, that so long as they stayed there, they were a threat to nobody, that our efforts should be addressed to the rich, populous lowlands.'

Krulak went on to state that if the enemy did leave the security of their hinterland bases and moved towards the populated coastal regions, 'they can be cut up by our supporting arms [artillery and aviation], the Marines are glad to take them on … but the real war is among the people and not among the mountains.'

General Vo Nguyen Giap, a senior commander of the NVA, confirmed Krulak's stance, writing: 'The primary emphasis is to draw American units into remote areas and thereby facilitate control of the population of the lowlands.'

The III MAF in Action (1966)

The III MAF's plan of battle for 1966, under General Walt's command, called for securing I Corps' coastal regions as well as conducting the search-and-destroy operation that Westmoreland wanted. III MAF's initial search-and-destroy operation, begun on 11 January, received the name Operation MALLARD. Unfortunately, the enemy formations that the plan sought to engage and destroy were nowhere to be found, except in small numbers. Operation MALLARD ended on 17 January.

At the end of 1965, Westmoreland had ordered the III MAF, in conjunction with the ARVN, to begin offensive operations along the border area between the southernmost province of I Corps and the northernmost province of II Corps, overseen by the US Army. The purpose was to stop an enemy build-up in that region. Receiving the name Operation DOUBLE EAGLE I, it took place between 28 January and 17 February 1966.

On 20 February Operation DOUBLE EAGLE II began and ran through to 1 March. In neither operation were enemy forces encountered in the large numbers expected, as the majority had withdrawn before the Marine/ARVN operations. The Marines claimed 324 enemy killed with the loss of 24 Marines. Lieutenant General Krulak concluded that, as had apparently happened during other Marine operations, the enemy had advance notice due to security breaches.

Krulak described several years later the poor impression that continuous search-and-destroy operations made on the South Vietnamese rural population, as the Marines 'would come in, comb the area and disappear; whereupon the VC would resurface and resume control.'

Operation DOUBLE EAGLE was followed by Operation UTAH, a combined Marine/ARVN endeavour. It lasted from 4 to 7 March. In this case, the NVA decided to stand and fight. The Marines claimed they accounted for 600 enemy dead and 7 captured. Marine losses came in at 98 killed and 278 wounded. The ARVN reported losses of 30 dead and 120 wounded.

Internal Dissent

From mid-May to early June of 1966, South Vietnam was wracked by severe religious and political strife, centred on the city of Da Nang and surrounding areas, bringing a temporary halt to ARVN military and pacification operations throughout the country.

At a number of points during the internal strife, rebel ARVN forces threatened local Marine units. In the end, the Marine leadership convinced the rebel leadership that this would not end well for them and the rebels backed down. A Marine officer much later expressed his fears to the Marine command when he stated:

> If we'd got ourselves in a position with the government forces fighting the local forces up there [Da Nang], and particularly if we had been caught in the middle of it and there'd been any significant US casualties, I have a feeling that the US Government would have probably pulled out of the war right then and there.

The Show Must Go On

The III MAF launched a pacification sweep-and-clear operation named Operation LIBERTY in and around the Da Nang air base. With limited ARVN support, it took place between 7 and 27 June. The enemy offered only minimal resistance, with the highest number of Marine losses attributed to mines.

From a publication titled *Small Unit Actions in Vietnam: Summer of 1966* appears this passage on the weaponry with which a Marine patrol went into battle:

> The Marines wore helmets and flak jackets. Each rifleman carried 150 rounds of ammunition and two or more hand grenades. The men of the two machine-gun crews were draped with belts of linked cartridges totaling 1,200 rounds. The two 3.5-inch rocket-launcher teams carried five high-explosive (HE) and five white phosphorus (WP) rockets. Four grenadiers carried twenty-eight 40mm shells apiece for their stubby M79s. Sergeant Cunningham had given six LAAWs [*sic*] to some riflemen to provide additional area target capability. Artillery and mortars were on call.

Marine Reconnaissance

In response to reports of a large NVA formation south of the Da Nang air base in early June, the III MAP ordered an extensive series of reconnaissance operations to pinpoint its locations. These missions involved Marines from either a division's reconnaissance battalion or a Force Command reconnaissance company. Both deployed behind enemy lines via helicopters. Whereas divisional reconnaissance units performed short-range tactical missions, those from the Force Command were intended for longer-range strategic purposes.

In the Medal of Honor citation of Gunnery Sergeant Jimmie E. Howard, platoon leader, Company C, First Reconnaissance Battalion, 1st Marine Division appears this extract describing his bravery on 16 June when his platoon, located on a mountain-top observation post (dubbed Hill 485), was attacked after midnight by an enemy battalion:

> Reacting swiftly and fearlessly in the face of the overwhelming odds, G/Sgt. Howard skillfully organized his small but determined force into a tight perimeter defense and calmly moved from position to position to direct his men's fire. When fragments of an exploding enemy grenade wounded him severely and prevented him from moving his legs, he distributed his ammunition to the remaining members of his platoon and proceeded to maintain radio communications and direct air strikes on the enemy with uncanny accuracy … G/Sgt. Howard was largely responsible for preventing the loss of his entire platoon.

When discovered by the enemy, or having completed their assignments, reconnaissance units were to be evacuated by helicopter. If required, they could be reinforced by a quick reaction team of varying sizes to aid in evacuation, as would be the case for Gunnery Sergeant Howard's platoon. A total of fifteen men in Howard's platoon received Silver Stars and two received the Navy Cross. The Battle for Hill 485 was part of a larger endeavour labelled Operation KANSAS that ran from 13 to 22 June.

The Enemy Crosses the DMZ

Beginning in early July 1966, Marine reconnaissance units began reporting the ever-growing presence of the NVA on the south (Marine) side of the DMZ. Prisoners captured by the ARVN confirmed this, indicating that the forces were of an NVA division. In response, the III MAF organized Operation HASTINGS to coincide with an ARVN operation unfolding south of the Marine operation. Operation HASTINGS began on 15 July and continued until 3 August.

The Marines of Operation HASTINGS, encountering the NVA main force, experienced fierce resistance, as reported in this passage by Staff Sergeant John J. McGinty:

> … we starting getting mortar fire, followed by automatic weapon fire from all sides … they were blowing bugles, and we could see them waving flags … 'Charlie' [the enemy] moved in waves with small arms right behind the mortars, and we estimated we were being attacked by a thousand men. We just couldn't kill them fast enough.

After heavy fighting on 18 July and the NVA's terrible losses from Marine supporting arms, the NVA became less interested in tangling with the Marine infantry units for a few days while they regrouped. There would be more bloody encounters between the Marines and the NVA on 24 and 25 July, with the last occurring on 28 July. With the conclusion of Operation HASTINGS, the Marines reported killing more than 700 enemy troops and capturing 17.

Marine casualties were also high – 126 killed and 448 wounded. Captain Robert J. Modrzejewski, receiving a Medal of Honor for his actions in repulsing numerous enemy attacks on his unit on 15 July, stated in the aftermath of the engagement: 'Our company was down from 130 to 80, and I had kids who were hit in five or six places.' ARVN losses were reported as twenty-one killed and forty wounded during their nearby but separate search-and-destroy operation.

Upon the conclusion of Operation HASTINGS, General Walt, III MAP commander, summed up his opinion of the NVA based on what had transpired:

> We found them well-equipped, well-trained, and aggressive to the point of fanaticism. They attacked in mass formations and died by the hundreds. Their leaders had misjudged the fighting ability of US Marines and ARVN soldiers together; our superiority in artillery and total command of the air. They had vastly underestimated…our [helicopter] mobility.

Follow-Up

Despite the success of Operation HASTINGS, General Westmoreland, MACV commander, believed that large NVA units still existed south of the DMZ and had to be addressed by the III MAF. This led to Operation PRAIRIE, which involved numerous reconnaissance Marine detachments sent to locate and engage these NVA units.

Operation PRAIRIE began on 3 August 1966. Three days later, the NVA started to react to the operation by going after a five-person reconnaissance team. The scope and ferocity escalated as more and more troops were fed in on both sides, only winding down four weeks later. The Marines claimed 200 enemy dead, while losing 37 killed and 130 wounded. The fighting picked up again the following month.

An impression of the fighting of late September appears in Captain Roger K. Ryman's appraisal of the Marines' foe, the NVA:

> Their fire discipline remained excellent. Invariably they'd pick just the right piece of terrain, where it was so narrow that we couldn't maneuver on the flanks, and they'd dig in and wait for us in the bottleneck. Sometimes they'd let the point man go by and then let us have it.

Marine Colonel Alexander D. Cereghino commented on the engagements in which he took part during the 1966 phase of Operation PRAIRIE: 'At the beginning of Prairie we were fighting well-trained and well-equipped soldiers. At the end, we were running into poorly-equipped young soldiers and frustrated commanders.'

Looking Back Over the Year

In spite of the fierce fighting during Operation PRAIRIE in 1966, the Marines of the III MAP took pride in knowing that they had prevented the NVA from establishing a major operating base south of the DMZ. Operation PRAIRIE itself would continue into December 1966, and then into early 1967 at a much reduced level of activity. The reason: the north-east monsoon season that lasted from October 1966 until March 1967.

A critical factor that allowed the Marine ground forces to prevail over the enemy in 1966 was their aerial support, both helicopter and fixed-wing. Marine helicopters flew over 400,000 sorties that year, with 75 per cent in support of the III MAP. Fifty-two helicopters were lost, with thirty-nine of those considered combat losses.

Not Going as Planned

In spite of the Marines' and US Army's 1966 successes in blunting their enemies' operations, the overall war was not going well for the American military. Robert S. McNamara, the civilian Secretary of Defense considered one of the early architects of America's involvement in the Vietnam War, had visited South Vietnam in 1966 and on 14 October 1966 he reported his impressions from that visit to American President Lyndon Johnson: 'There is no sign of an impending break in enemy morale, and it appears that he can more than replace his losses … Pacification is a bad disappointment … full security exists nowhere – not even behind Marine lines and in Saigon; in the countryside, the enemy almost completely controls the night.'

The fixed-wing assets of Marine aviation in 1966 flew over 60,000 sorties. Of that number, 43,000 were in direct support of the III MAP. The other 17,000 sorties were flown by Marine aviation in support of the Seventh Air Force campaign over both South and North Vietnam, as well as the neighbouring country of Laos. The Seventh Air Force was the Air Component Command of the MACV. The cost to Marine aviation in 1966 came to fifty-one aircraft.

The 1st Marine Division in Action (1967)

With the beginning of 1967, the 1st Marine Division found itself hard-pressed for manpower as it would be involved in a three-pronged war effort. At the infantry company level and below, it conducted untold thousands of patrols. These sought to deter enemy attacks on friendly industrial and military sites within the three southern-most provinces of I Corps, as well as protect the civilian population residing in the coastal regions.

Second, the 1st Marine Division tried to provide as much support as possible for the South Vietnamese government's efforts to neutralize the enemy's political/military infrastructure in I Corps' coastal regions. Well aware of the threat posed, the enemy constantly interfered with South Vietnamese government 'Revolutionary Development Teams'. The American CIA established the original programme in 1964.

Last, the 1st Marine Division went about conducting infantry battalion-sized or more extensive operations against VC main force units that might pose a threat to the three southernmost provinces of I Corps. The first four of these – labelled Operation DESOTO, DECKHOUSE VI, UNION and UNION II – all took place between January and June 1967.

Such was the demand for additional Marines during these operations that the US Army tasked its 23rd Infantry Division, better known as the 'Americal' Division, with responsibility for security in the two southernmost provinces of I Corps, allowing the 1st Marine Division to concentrate in the central province of I Corps. This restructuring, called 'Task Force Oregon', took place between April and September of 1967. The III MAF, despite the 23rd being a US Army unit, had oversight over the 23rd's operations.

Operation UNION II

A description of fighting during Operation UNION II in June 1967 appears in this extract from the Medal of Honor citation of Captain James Albert Graham:

> Company F, a leading company, was proceeding across a clear rice paddy area 1,000 meters wide, attacking towards the assigned objective, when it came under fire from mortars and small arms which immediately inflicted a large number of casualties. Hardest hit by the enemy fire was the 2nd platoon of

Company F, which was pinned down in the open paddy area by intense fire from two concealed machine guns. Forming an assault unit from members of his small company, Captain Graham boldly led a fierce assault … forcing the enemy to abandon the first machine gun … Resolute to silence the second machine gun, which continued its devastating fire, Capt. Graham's small force stood steadfast in its hard-won enclave.

In June 1967, Lieutenant General Robert E. Cushman replaced Lieutenant General Lewis W. Walt as the III MAF commander. Cushman had served as the deputy commander of III MAF between April and May 1967 and, like Walt, he was a highly-decorated veteran of the Second World War.

They Never Stopped Coming

In spite of their heavy losses during January through to June 1967, the enemy never wavered in their commitment to complete victory. They continued to send more troops into the three southern provinces in I Corps to battle the US Marine 1st Division, US Army 23rd Division and ARVN divisions.

In early July 1967, a VC main force unit mounted a successful attack on a large South Vietnamese prison located within I Corps. They managed to breach the jail's defences and freed 1,196 military and political prisoners.

On 14 July, the enemy fired fifty long-range 122mm rockets into the Da Nang air base, destroying ten aircraft and damaging another forty. The Marines, in response, enlarged their defensive belt around the air base. The number of Marine overflights was also significantly increased, to detect and destroy enemy rocket teams. In spite of these measures, the rocket attacks still continued.

The deputy commander of MACV, Major General Raymond L. Murray, remarked on the complications posed by rockets: 'It [the enemy rocket capacity] was constantly on everybody's mind. With a relatively minor investment in men and equipment, the NVA could keep an entire Marine division occupied.'

After detecting an NVA regiment operating in the southernmost province of I Corps in late July 1967, plans were quickly put forward to engage and destroy it, in conjunction with the ARVN mounting a companion operation. The 1st Marine Division portion received the name Operation COCHISE and began on 8 August, continuing until 28 August. The combined Marine/ARVN operations forced the NVA regiment to relocate, but it retained its fighting capability.

At the beginning of September 1967, the NVA returned in divisional strength. In response, the Marines mounted Operation SWIFT on 4 September. During the first few days of the operation, the NVA engaged various Marine infantry units and inflicted severe losses. As almost always, it proved to be the Marine supporting arms that turned the tide of battle.

Nothing Really Changes

Operation SWIFT ended on 15 September, only to be followed by numerous other operations of varying sizes throughout I Corps that continued until the end of 1967. Many aimed to protect Da Nang air base simply by keeping the enemy far enough away so that their rocket teams could not strike it.

An example of what the 1st Marine Division encountered in their efforts to clear their portion of I Corps occurred when a Marine infantry company took on the assignment of seizing an NVA fortified village during Operation ESSEX. It unfolded between 6 and 17 November. Describing the incident in 1981, Lieutenant Colonel Gene W. Bowers stated:

> The [Marine] assault was well coordinated and executed, maintaining continuous fire superiority over the enemy until the assault line reached the bamboo hedgerow on the periphery of the village. Eight taut strands of US[-type] barbed wire were unexpectedly encountered woven among the bamboo stalks. As the Marines fought to break through the barrier, .50 caliber machine-gun fire from 800 meters on the right flank and 800 meters on the left flank commenced enfilading, grazing fire down the line of barbed wire as 60mm, 82mm and 4.2in mortar rounds began impacting in the [rice] paddy before the village. Our platoon commander, Second Lieutenant Robert W. Miller, Jr, was killed and both platoon sergeants were severely wounded. The assault faltered, and the Marines took cover, protected by small inter-paddy dikes.

The 3d Marine Division in Action (1967)

In the two relatively unpopulated northern I Corps provinces that faced the DMZ, the 3d Marine Division found itself as anticipated engaged in large-scale battles with elements from more than four NVA divisions. These began in January 1967 and grew in scope and intensity in the summer and autumn.

General Westmoreland had outlined the threat to the northernmost provinces of I Corps in a 13 September 1966 message to his US Navy counterpart: 'The seriousness of the threat underscores the importance and urgency of utilizing all practicable means to prevent the enemy from generating a major offensive designed to liberate the provinces in question and to inflict maximum casualties.'

Operation PRAIRIE

According to the Marines, during August 1996 through to January 1967, Operation PRAIRIE accounted for 1,397 enemy soldiers killed and 27 captured. Marine losses came in at 239 dead and 1,214 wounded.

Due to the success of Operation PRAIRIE, I Corps decided to mount Operation PRAIRIE II, in conjunction with local ARVN units, on 1 February 1967. Running until

18 March, like its namesake, its goal was the destruction of any NVA forces operating south of the DMZ.

Due to an increasingly massive build-up of enemy forces and their artillery north of the DMZ, the 3d Marine Division obtained permission (for the first time) on 25 February to deliver artillery fire across the DMZ. The action resulted in heavy NVA counter-battery artillery fire beginning on 27 February.

NVA ground units also began mounting operations south of the DMZ in response. In one engagement they successfully ambushed a Marine column. In 1981 then Marine Major Robert F. Sheridan recounted a brief description of the events leading to an NVA ambush of his unit:

> We were ordered to proceed … knowing full well we were walking into a hornets' nest. Based on the number of enemy forces we had already encountered and the vast amount of equipment, new weapons and ammunition, we knew we were outnumbered and outgunned … We left the perimeter … and within 200 yards we came upon a huge radio complex. The trail was narrow, and we could not disperse our troops. One could almost smell the enemy force.

As the Marines poured more assets into the battle, they eventually gained the advantage in firepower, pushing the NVA into withdrawal. In the closing stages of Operation PRAIRIE II, the Marines came across enemy mass grave sites. The Marines claimed 694 enemy troops killed and 20 captured, while 93 Marines died in the fighting, with another 483 wounded.

Operation PRAIRIE III and IV

On 19 March the Marines along the DMZ began Operation PRAIRIE III, which continued until 19 April. At one point the NVA attacked a Marine company command post guarded by a platoon of infantry. In the Medal of Honor citation of Second Lieutenant John Paul Bobo appears the following passage:

> When an exploding enemy mortar round severed Lieutenant Bobo's right leg below the knee, he refused to be evacuated and insisted upon being placed in a firing position to cover the movement of the command group to a better location. With a web belt around his leg serving as a tourniquet and with his leg jammed into the dirt to curtail the bleeding, he remained in his position and delivered devastating fire into the ranks of the enemy attempting to overrun the Marines. Lieutenant Bobo was mortally wounded while firing his weapon into the main point of the enemy attack.

By the time Operation PRAIRIE III ended, the Marines had once again pushed the NVA back across the DMZ. In the process, they claimed an enemy body count of 252 killed and 4 captured. The Marine losses were 56 dead and 530 wounded.

Despite the NVA's failed attempts to push across the DMZ in early 1967, they continued to build up and push ever larger forces south across the DMZ into South Vietnam during the summer and autumn of that year.

The Fighting Continues

On 10 May, a worrying event occurred for Marine aviation. An A-4 Skyhawk was taking part in a ground-support mission along the South Vietnamese side of the DMZ. It encountered enemy surface-to-air missiles (SAMs) that brought the aircraft down. Before this event, Marine pilots had met only various types of anti-aircraft guns in South Vietnam.

Following Operation PRAIRIE III, the Marines began Operation PRAIRIE IV. The NVA also went on the offensive at the same time, trying on 13 May to overrun an important Marine position at Con Thien, less than 2 miles from the DMZ.

The enemy's attack on Con Thien included an ambush of the joint Marine and US Army relief column. Despite the NVA's best efforts, Marine supporting firepower again proved their undoing and resulted in their loss of 197 men killed and 8 captured. The Marines listed 44 of their own killed and 110 wounded.

The Rules Change

The Marines had not been allowed to enter the DMZ for fear that they might mistakenly cross it. This greatly hampered effective operations as it allowed the NVA a buffer zone in the DMZ that was safe from American attack. The day after the NVA's initial attack from the buffer zone against Con Thien, the American government lifted the ban.

To take advantage of the change in rules, the Marines planned divisional-sized operations to begin on 18 May in conjunction with an ARVN division. The aim was to clear the NVA from the former buffer area. To prevent civilian losses, the South Vietnam National Police evacuated approximately 12,000 non-combatants from the field before the start of various operations.

The Marines keep at it

Instead of a single name, the new operations aimed at clearing out the former buffer zone of the NVA would receive individual names reflecting a variety of geographic areas and different Marine and ARVN units; hence there was Operation HICKORY, Operation LAM SON 54, Operation BELT TIGHT and Operation BEAU CHARGER.

The last of the operations concluded on 28 May. Estimated enemy losses came in at 789 killed and 37 captured. Recorded Marine casualties were 142 dead and 896 wounded. The ARVN listed 22 killed and 122 injured. Both sides' claims of the number of enemy losses often proved overstated to appear more successful than was actually the case.

Following the various operations aimed at clearing the NVA from the buffer zone, the participating Marine and ARVN units joined in finishing off Operation PRAIRIE IV, which officially ended on 31 May 1967. NVA losses came in at 508 dead and 8 captured, with friendly casualties placed at 164 killed and 1,240 wounded.

To keep the enemy on the run, the day after Operation PRAIRIE IV ended, Operation CIMARRON began with the same Marine and ARVN units sweeping the same area. However, the NVA had wisely decided that they had suffered enough and through to 2 July, the last day of Operation CIMARRON, they offered little resistance. There then began Operation BUFFALO.

The Enemy Goes on the Offensive

As Operation BUFFALO unfolded, the NVA mounted a significant offensive against Con Thien once again. An important outpost for US forces, its capture by the enemy would be a decisive victory as it would open up a key route for the NVA to insert into South Vietnam 35,000 troops already staged on the north side of the DMZ.

The NVA's second significant attempt to seize Con Thien began near the outpost at the beginning of Operation BUFFALO. Two Marine infantry companies un-knowingly walked into a large-scale enemy ambush and ran into a firestorm of enemy fire. When the Marines attempted to take cover from the intense fire, the enemy employed flame-throwers to force them into the open where their small-arms fire decimated the now-exposed Marines.

In hurried support of the two hard-hit Marine infantry companies, Marine aviation dropped 90 tons of ordnance in the first few hours. A Marine staff sergeant later stated: 'I asked for napalm as close as 50 yards from us; some of it came in only 20 yards away. But I'm not complaining.' Besides Marine artillery and tanks, US Navy destroyers added their firepower to the battle. When the fighting finally concluded with a Marine withdrawal, the Marines had lost 84 dead, 190 wounded and 9 missing. Enemy losses were unknown.

In answer to the ever-present threat from Marine aviation, the enemy moved more SAMs into the area south of the DMZ, accounting for another Marine jet fighter on 6 July. Enemy artillery fire from across the DMZ also became more accurate during this time as demonstrated on 7 July with a direct hit on a Marine command post. It was determined to be a 152mm high-explosive (HE) round that had struck and penetrated the well-protected bunker.

As had happened so many times before, Marine supporting arms broke the back of the NVA summer offensive operation against the base at Con Thien. This had been the enemy's most substantial push across the DMZ up until that time, with the enemy calling it quits on or around 8 July 1967. Operation BUFFALO concluded on 14 July 1967. The Marines claimed they had accounted for 1,290 enemy soldiers killed and 2 captured. Marine losses came in at 159 killed and 345 wounded.

The McNamara Line

Under discussion at the highest levels of the US government since March 1966 was the idea of creating some unmanned barrier system along the southern boundary of the DMZ, including mines and various types of sensors, to help contain the NVA. Marine aviation would support this defensive line. The man behind the concept was Robert S. McNamara, the civilian Secretary of Defense.

A senior US Navy admiral pointed out on 13 September 1966 the disadvantage of installing an unmanned defensive line along the DMZ: '… a barrier system must be tended; if not, it could be breached with ease, while the flow of men and the material to the VC/NVA continued.'

The commander of the 3d Marine Division agreed, saying that the entire concept was 'absurd'. In the end, on 15 September 1966, the barrier system, now to include Marine-manned strongpoints, was ordered built.

Extremely costly to construct, the barrier system went by several official names but eventually came to be known, unofficially, by the Marines as the 'McNamara Line'. The emphasis on its construction began to wane in January 1968, and officially ended in October 1968 as other more pressing concerns arose.

The McNamara Line ended up as a costly failure and proved to be a burden on the manpower and equipment of the III MAP – especially the 3d Marine Division – at a very trying time.

Lieutenant General Cushman, appointed the commander of the III MAP in June 1967, recalled in 1982: '… really got in a fit with some of the engineer [US Army] colonels that would come roaring up from Saigon to see how the fence was doing and … I'd say "Well it's going fine, go up and take a look", which they always did. Always had a few people around, but we just weren't going out getting everybody killed building that stupid fence.'

One unnamed Marine officer stated his opinion of the McNamara Line and its value: 'With these bastards [the NVA], you'd have to build the [barrier] zone all the way to India, and it would take the whole Marine Corps and half the [US] Army to guard it; even then they'd probably burrow under it.'

Second Attempt by the NVA

The NVA would not give up on Con Thien. The Marines had their first indication that the enemy was going to try again in late August 1967, as the intensity of NVA artillery and rocket fire significantly increased with the primary target being Con Thien. The enemy required a propaganda victory before the north-east monsoon season began.

On 3 September, the NVA once again crossed the DMZ in force, with their main thrust to the south and south-east of Con Thien. The Marines beat these attacks back in hard fighting, requiring the largest concentration of firepower during the Vietnam

War in support of a single division. Taking part in this demonstration of American military muscle, besides Marine Corps supporting arms, were US Air Force planes including B-52 bombers.

Despite enduring an unheard-of amount of punishment, the enemy threat to Con Thien continued until the end of December 1967. An example of NVA persistence is described in this extract by Lieutenant Colonel John C. Studt in 1981, representing the fighting in late October during the closing stages of Operation KINGFISHER:

> From before dusk … until almost 0200 in the morning, we were under almost continuous attack by both direct and indirect fire, and our perimeter was hit again and again by ground attacks … The wounded were being accumulated in the vicinity of my CP [command post], which consisted of foxholes, and the suffering was a cause of anguish. After several attempts to medevac them by helicopter were aborted due to intense enemy fire, we came up with the plan that on signal every man on the perimeter would open fire on known or suspected enemy positions … for a few minutes with an intense volume of fire. During this brief period, a volunteer pilot … succeeded in zipping into the zone and removing our emergency medevacs. The [trick] … probably would have not worked again.

Concerned about the continuing threat posed by the NVA to the DMZ, General Westmoreland deployed a 1st Cavalry Division brigade to the area around the Da Nang air base in October 1967. This allowed the III MAF commander to move a 1st Marine Division regiment to the northernmost province of I Corps in support of the hard-pressed 3d Marine Division. The repositioning of the 1st and 3d Marine divisions in the autumn of 1967 closer to the DMZ to foil predicted 1968 NAV offensives would become known as Operation CHECKERS.

Self-Defeating Policy Issue

Despite the 3d Marine Division's hard-won success in turning back the NVA divisions' two significant attempts to cross the DMZ into South Vietnam in 1967, there was no pursuit by I Corps divisions back across the line to finish off those retreating divisions. US government policy at the time did not allow such actions for fear of provoking a hostile reaction from the Red Chinese and Soviet governments and a possible widening of the conflict.

Marine Brigadier General Louis Metzger, who later became assistant commander of the 3d Marine Division, later expressed the disdain that he and other Marines had had for the policy of not being able to pursue retreating enemy across the DMZ in the summer and fall of 1967:

> It has long been my belief that the most significant aspect of operation along the DMZ was the publicly-stated United States policy that US Forces would not

Victory is Just around the Corner

General Westmoreland, MACV commander, stated in November 1967: 'Infiltration will slow; the Communist infrastructure will be cut up and near collapse; the Vietnamese Government will prove its stability, and the Vietnamese army will show that it can handle the Vietcong; United States units can begin to phase down.'

enter North Vietnam. This allowed the enemy to deploy his forces across the DMZ at the time and place of his choosing, and to withdraw to a sanctuary when it suited his convenience; to utilize his artillery against US positions and bases while at the same time denying the Marines the most effective means of destroying the enemy weapons.

A Look Back at 1967

In turning back enemy incursions across the DMZ in 1967, the 3d Marine Division suffered a large number of casualties, especially during the fighting around Con Thien, which totalled 956 men. Losses for the year totalled approximately 5,000 dead and wounded. Marine Lieutenant General Victor H. Krulak, commander of FMF/Pac, and his US Navy counterpart agreed that such a loss rate was not sustainable.

Krulak would go on to state that the enemy's purpose in 1967 was as follows:

> … to get us as near to his weapons and to his forces as possible, drench us with high-angle fire weapons, engage us in close and violent combat, accept willingly a substantial loss of life for the opportunity to kill a lesser number of our men, and to withdraw into his North Vietnam sanctuary to refurbish.

A Marine Corps M48A3 medium tank disembarks from a US Navy landing craft. The bulk of the 1st Marine Division arrived in South Vietnam during the first half of 1966. The division would be stood up in July 1966 and assigned the security of the three southernmost provinces of I Corps. In October 1966, the 3d Marine Division took responsibility for the two northernmost provinces of I Corps. (*USMC*)

In South Vietnam, the III MAF served under the oversight of Military Assistance Command, Vietnam (MACV). Its commander from August 1964 through to 1968 would be US Army four-star General William C. Westmoreland, pictured here. He firmly believed that American military forces could win the Vietnam War by attrition, using its firepower advantage over the Viet Cong and North Vietnamese Army (NVA). (*US Army*)

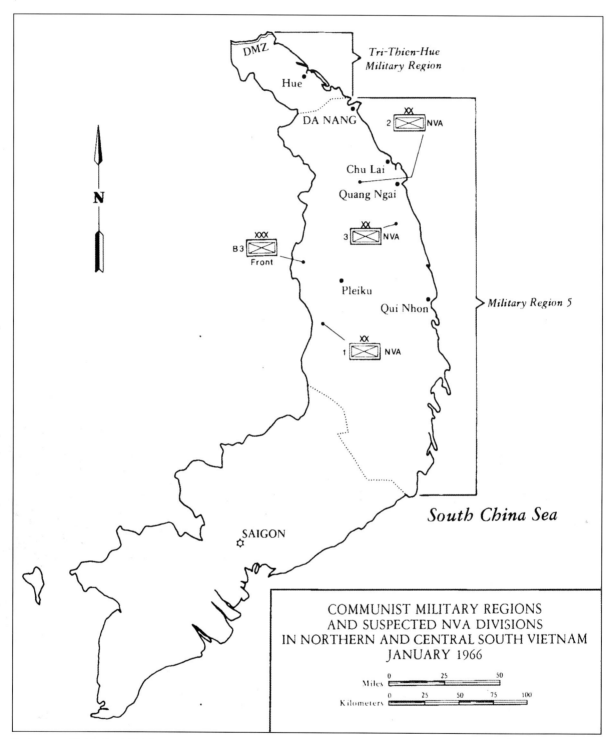

COMMUNIST MILITARY REGIONS
AND SUSPECTED NVA DIVISIONS
IN NORTHERN AND CENTRAL SOUTH VIETNAM
JANUARY 1966

By January 1966, the NVA had three divisions as seen from this map in South Vietnam. It had also begun amassing large numbers of troops and equipment just north of the Demilitarized Zone (DMZ) that separated North and South Vietnam. Westmoreland wanted the III MAF to concentrate on the destruction of NVA divisions in I Corps, rather than the Marine preference for concentrating on pacification efforts. *(USMC)*

Marine three-star Lieutenant General Victor H. Krulak, pictured here, was a veteran of both the Second World War and the Korean War, and a specialist in counter-insurgency warfare. During the Vietnam War he oversaw the Fleet Marine Force/Pacific (FMF/Pac). In that command slot Krulak could only exercise administrative command of the III MAF, such as selecting its personnel, replacements and so forth. (USMC)

As the III MAF grew in size later during 1965 and 1966, it devoted increasing resources to pacification efforts aimed at winning the hearts and minds of the South Vietnamese people. In just the area around the Da Nang air base, there were 150,000 civilians within 81mm mortar range. One reliable way of convincing the local population of the Marines' good intentions was by providing medical care. (USMC)

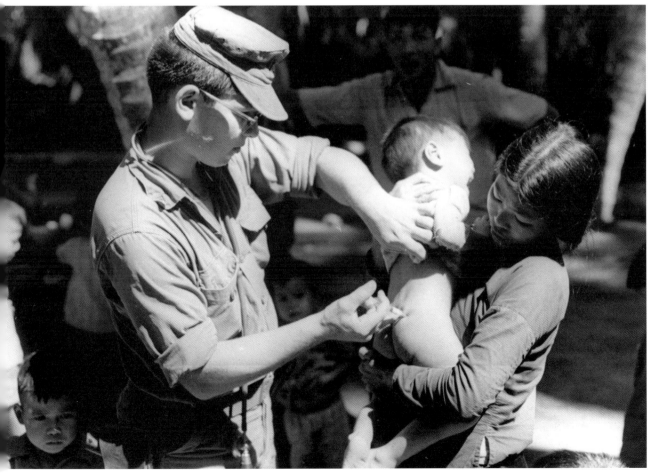

(**Above**) Due to the ebb and flow of the III MAF's combat operations in I Corps, the rural population often had to be uprooted. Once in resettlement camps, they lacked access to food, clothing and shelter. To ease their suffering, the Marines contacted private charitable organizations to donate the much-needed items. Pictured here is a Marine helping a civilian to transport a sack of rice. (*USMC*)

(**Opposite, above**) The III MAF operations were hampered in early 1966, as were the enemy's, by heavy monsoon rains that ran roughly from October 1965 to the following March in central South Vietnam. In this picture, a rain-soaked Marine is wearing a US Navy wet-weather parka and using an AN/PRC-25 field radio. The makeshift tent appears to consist of rubberized ponchos tied together. (*USMC*)

(**Opposite, below**) Waiting for orders is a no doubt very wet and miserable Marine rifleman keeping watch on his surroundings, armed with an M14 rifle. Of note is that the Marine pictured here is not wearing his M1 steel helmet. Rather, he is wearing only the fibre lining from his helmet for protection from the elements. Around his waist is the 1961 rifle belt and accoutrements supported by the M1941 belt suspenders. (*USMC*)

A Marine rifleman with his M1911A1 .45 calibre automatic pistol at the ready. Typically, the only enlisted men authorized with handguns were those assigned to crew-served weapons. The Marine pictured here is wearing the M1955 body armour unofficially nicknamed the 'flak vest'. The Marine Corps had first issued body armour to its men during the Korean War. (*USMC*)

(**Opposite, above**) Loaded, the M14 rifle pictured here in the arms of two Marine infantrymen weighed 10.7lb and fired a powerful 7.62mm round with an effective range of up to 500 yards. The Marine in the foreground, besides carrying a binoculars case, is wearing on his waist belt an M1956 universal small-arms ammunition pouch. (*USMC*)

(**Opposite, below**) The M14 seen in the hands of this Marine rifleman during the Vietnam War was a semi-automatic weapon. In theory each Marine fire team had a single man armed with a selective-fire version of the rifle labelled the M14A1. It had a practical rate of fire in fully-automatic mode of sixty rounds per minute. The M14 rifle series would be the American military's last so-called 'battle rifle' or 'full-power combat rifle'. (*USMC*)

(**Right**) Humping a crate of ammunition, this Marine rifleman has two M26 fragmentation grenades attached to his flak vest. The grenade had a smooth sheet-metal body and a serrated wire coil within, which broke into many fragments upon detonation. The blast radius of the M26 came in at approximately 33ft. (*USMC*)

(**Opposite, above left**) The Viet Cong and NVA soldiers were supplied with a variety of Soviet and Chinese-built weapons. Pictured here, a Marine holds up for the photographer a Soviet-supplied RKG-3 anti-tank grenade. Once thrown at its intended target, a parachute would pop out from the base, orientating it so that the 'top' would point to the armoured fighting vehicle. On striking, a firing pin would travel 'up' the handle to the detonator. (*USMC*)

(**Opposite, above right**) Not always able to depend on a reliable supply of hand grenades or mines, the Viet Cong became masters of creating a wide array of improvised explosive devices. In this picture, we see an improvised hand grenade made from a discarded soda can. The explosives that filled such weapons came from unexploded American ordnance scavenged from battlefields. (*USMC*)

(**Opposite, below**) Seen here in South Vietnam is a Marine Corps Self-Propelled M109 155mm Howitzer. The original plans for the vehicle called for it to replace all the towed M114A1 155mm howitzers in the Marine 1965 divisional TO&E. However, funding shortfalls prevented that from occurring and resulted in only one battery in the division being equipped with it. (*USMC*)

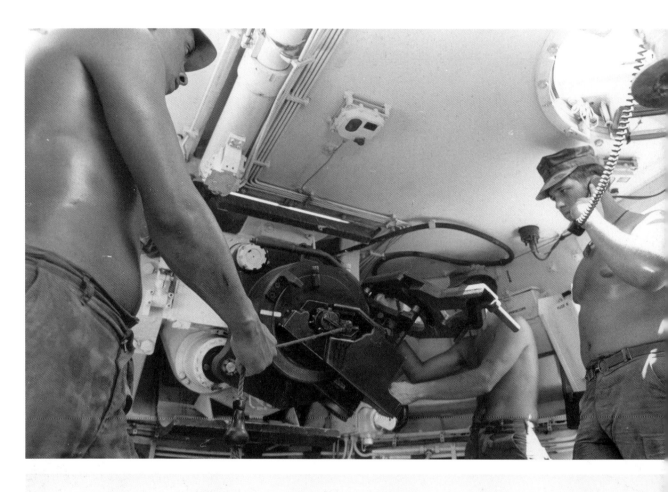

(**Opposite, above**) The interior of a Marine Corps Self-Propelled M109 155mm Howitzer in South Vietnam. The M109 was crewed by six men: vehicle commander, gunner, driver and three ammunition-handlers. The shirtless crew reflects the fact that there was no onboard air-conditioning system. The vehicle was constructed of thin welded aluminium armour offering protection only from some types of small-arms fire and artillery fragments. (*USMC*)

(**Opposite, below**) A Marine Corps M53 155mm self-propelled gun during the Vietnam War. Classified as a heavy artillery piece, it was not organic to the Marine divisional level but allocated from the next higher command level, referred to as 'Force Troops'. It had appeared in Marine Corps' service after the Korean War. The vehicle rode on various components of the M47 and M48 medium tanks. (*USMC*)

(**Above**) The counterpart of the M53 155mm self-propelled gun in Marine Corps' service was the M55 8in (203mm) self-propelled howitzer pictured here. It had the same chassis and turret as the M53. The weapons, in theory, could be interchanged between vehicles. The 8in howitzer lacked the 155mm gun's range but proved to be more accurate. (*Author's collection*)

(**Opposite, above**) The 8in self-propelled howitzer M110 shown here replaced the M55 8in (203mm) self-propelled howitzer in Marine service during the Vietnam War. The 8in howitzer's thick barrel was 17ft 10in in length and weighed 8,490lb. It could fire a 229lb HE round out to a maximum range of approximately 27,000 yards. (*Author's collection*)

(**Opposite, below**) Found at both Marine divisional and Force Troop level were reconnaissance elements. Those of the latter, known as 'Recon Marines', had a superior skill set compared to those at the divisional level. In the field, Marine reconnaissance members tended to be face-painted as is seen in this photograph and wore short-brim headgear, unofficially nicknamed 'boonie hats', instead of helmets. (*USMC*)

(**Above**) The Viet Cong guerrillas often had to make do with whatever small arms were available, as seen here with the man in the foreground of the photograph armed with an American-made Browning automatic rifle (BAR) M1918A2. Their diverse mixture of small arms came from a wide variety of sources including the Soviet Union and Red China, plus captured French and ARVN small arms. (*USMC*)

(**Above**) Shown here are three interesting submachine guns captured from the Viet Cong by the Marines. The uppermost is a Soviet PPS-42 dating from the Second World War. The weapon in the middle is, of course, the famous German MP 40, and the weapon on the bottom the K-50M. The latter was a Viet Cong modified version of the Red Chinese Army Type 50 submachine gun. (*USMC*)

(**Opposite, above**) Here, a young Marine displays small arms captured from the Viet Cong. In either hand he is holding a French-designed and built MAT-49 submachine gun that had first appeared in French Army use in 1949. The weapon on the left is a Second World War Soviet-designed Model 1944 carbine. The Red Chinese Army post-war-built copy became the Type 53. (*USMC*)

(**Opposite, below left**) Pictured here is a Soviet-designed and built Tokarev Model TT-33 automatic pistol captured by the Marine Corps in South Vietnam. Fitted with an eight-round detachable box magazine, the pistol's mechanism is based on the American-designed and built M1911 automatic pistol. Whereas the American weapon fired a .45 calibre round, the Tokarev fired a 7.62mm round. (*USMC*)

(**Opposite, below right**) Among the many types of enemy weaponry captured by the Marines during the Vietnam War was the Soviet-designed and built LPO-50 man-portable flame-thrower. Weighing in at approximately 50lb, it contained about 21lb of fuel fired in short bursts out to a range of between 55 to 76 yards. Like all man-portable flame-throwers, the weapon's accuracy depended on the range to a target and wind conditions. (*USMC*)

Marines are posing here with a captured enemy 82mm mortar and ammunition. Note the Marine on the left-hand side of the photograph demonstrating the method by which the enemy transported mortar rounds. The weapon itself is Soviet-designed and built and first saw service in the Second World War. It bore the designation 82-BM-37. (*USMC*)

(**Opposite, above left**) In this staged photo, a South Vietnamese civilian has been pressed into portraying a Viet Cong soldier hiding inside a tunnel. He is holding a Soviet-designed SKS semi-automatic carbine. Those possessed by the Viet Cong and NVA were either original Soviet-built examples or Red Chinese copies. It was a semi-automatic weapon only. (*US Army*)

(**Opposite, above right**) In another staged shot, a South Vietnamese civilian has been made up to look like an NVA soldier with a 7.62mm AK-47 assault rifle. As with the SKS carbine, those employed by the enemy were either original Soviet-built examples or Red Chinese copies designated the Type 56-1. The Chinese copy had a permanent folding bayonet underneath the muzzle, which the Soviet-built example did not. (*US Army*)

(**Opposite, below left**) The American-designed and built replacement for the M14 rifle during the Vietnam War would be the M16 selective-fire rifle pictured here in the hands of a wounded Marine. They first appeared in Marine Corps' service in South Vietnam in 1967. Unlike the M14 that fired a much larger 7.62mm round, the M16 was chambered to fire a smaller 5.56mm round. (*USMC*)

(**Opposite, below right**) Due to production issues, the M16 rifle's initial entry into service during the Vietnam War proved a disaster. It had not helped that the manufacturer of the weapon had stressed that it did not need cleaning. Once that misconception had been cleared up, the Marines (and US Army soldiers) were issued with cleaning kits and directed to clean their weapons as often as possible. (*USMC*)

(**Above**) For many of the older generation of Marines that had trained on the large and heavy M1 Garand rifle and then the M14 with the typical wooden stocks, the much smaller and lighter plastic-like M16 reminded them of a toy gun. This resulted in the unofficial nickname of the 'Mattel' after the well-known toy company of the day. (*USMC*)

(**Opposite, above**) Here a Marine rifleman is comparing the size of a captured AK-47 with his M16 rifle. The M16 was originally issued with a twenty-round box magazine that was later replaced with a thirty-round version to match the thirty-round magazine capacity of the AK-47. In 1969 the M16 was, in turn, the re-designed and improved M16A1 rifle. (*USMC*)

(**Opposite, below**) The Marine Corps had relied on a variety of different Landing Vehicles Tracked (LVTs) to transport its men from ship to shore during the Second World War. In the early 1950s, the Marines took into service a family of new LVTs, one of which would be the LVTP5 pictured here. The letter prefix 'P' in the vehicle's designation stood for 'personnel'. (*USMC*)

(**Opposite, above**) Two LVTP5s during the Vietnam War. Most Marines felt safer riding on top of the vehicles due to the fear of enemy mines exploding against the vehicle's gasoline tanks located in its floor. The vehicle's sole armament consisted of a small one-man turret armed with a .30 calibre machine gun. The 8,600lb amphibious tractor had a three-man crew and could transport up to twenty-five men from ship to shore or up to thirty-five men on land. (*USMC*)

(**Above**) To recover disabled LVTP5s, a recovery version of the vehicle would be built and receive the designation LVTR1 ('R' for 'recovery'). There were also a small number of engineering versions of the LVTP5 constructed to clear minefields and beach obstacles labelled the LVTE1. They have a large full-width mine plough mounted on the front of the vehicle, as seen in this Vietnam War photograph. (*USMC*)

(**Opposite, below**) Another variant in the LVTP5 series would be the LVTH6 ('H' for 'Howitzer') pictured here. Armament consisted of a turret-mounted 105mm howitzer and a coaxial .30 calibre machine gun. The vehicle's mission involved providing fire support for the other variants in the series during landing operations. The thickest armour on the vehicle would be 25mm on the front of the turret. (*Patton Museum*)

(**Above**) The Marine Corps M48A3 medium tanks pictured here had diesel engines and entered service in late 1964. Armament consisted of a 90mm main gun and several machine guns. Appreciated by those who served in them in South Vietnam was its thick lower hull armour that protected its crew from the majority of enemy mines and improvised explosive devices (IEDs). (*USMC*)

(**Opposite, above**) Seen here in service with the Marine Corps during the Vietnam War is the M67A2 flame-thrower tank. Based on the M48A3 medium tank, the vehicle's 90mm main gun was replaced by a flame gun tube. That tube had a phony blast deflector and bore an evacuator to disguise its purpose. (*USMC*)

(**Opposite, below**) To perform maintenance on the Marine Corps' armoured vehicles during the Vietnam War, the Marines employed the heavy recovery vehicle M51 pictured here. It has just removed the engine of an M48A3 medium tank. Based on the chassis of the M103 heavy tank series, production of the M51 began in 1954 and ended the following year with 187 units completed (104 initially for the Marine Corps). (*USMC*)

(**Opposite, above**) The preferred close-support aircraft of the Marine Corps during the Vietnam War proved to be the A-4 Skyhawk pictured here. It was small and very manoeuvrable, making it a harder target for enemy anti-aircraft gunners to acquire and hit, and it could deliver a wide variety of weapons ranging from bombs to napalm. The biggest drawback was its limited payload of approximately 3,000lb. (*USMC*)

(**Above**) As useful as the A-4 Skyhawk was in the close-support role for the Marine Corps during the Vietnam War, the much larger and heavier F-4 Phantom II pictured here was considered a more versatile aircraft. Primarily designed as an interceptor in the air-to-air role, its payload capacity of up to 8,000lb made it extremely useful in the secondary role of close support. (*USMC*)

(**Opposite, below**) A total of eleven Marine Corps squadrons flew the F-4 Phantom between 1965 and 1973 during the Vietnam War. The majority of the squadrons flew from land air bases such as Da Nang and Chu Lai in South Vietnam, as well as the Nam Phong air base in Thailand. The aircraft's most potent bomb was the 1,000lb Mk. 83 employed primarily against enemy underground facilities. (*USMC*)

(**Opposite, above**) Here in the foreground is a Marine F-4 Phantom II and in the background an A-4F Skyhawk during the Vietnam War. The latter has a dorsal hump that contained extra avionics. It also received a more powerful engine. A total of 147 units of the A-4F came off the assembly lines. Eventually, the majority of A-4Es employed in South Vietnam were brought up to the A-4F standard. (*USMC*)

(**Opposite, below**) In 1967 the first squadron of Marine A-6 Intruders arrived in South Vietnam. As the only all-weather/night-attack aircraft in the Marine Corps' inventory, it performed numerous interdiction missions over North Vietnam and South Vietnam as well as Laos. With a payload capacity of approximately 18,000lb, it could carry a wide variety of weapons as seen in this picture. (*US Navy*)

(**Above**) A variant of the F-4 Phantom II series that first showed up in South Vietnam in Marine Corps' service in 1966 would be the RF-4 pictured here at the Da Nang air base. The prefix letter 'R' in the designation stood for 'reconnaissance'. The RF-4 would be the replacement for the RF-8A photo reconnaissance plane based on the F-8 Crusader interceptor. (*USMC*)

The bulk of the 1st MAW spent its time during the Vietnam War at the massive Da Nang air base pictured here. The revetments provided a degree of protection from enemy mortar and rocket fire. The French first built an airfield near the city of Da Nang in the 1930s. During the American military's time in South Vietnam, it housed both Marine and USAF squadrons. (*USAF*)

As American military air power proved to be the most dangerous threat, the Viet Cong and NVA targeted the Da Nang air base as often as possible with ground attacks as well as mortar and rocket attacks. A Marine is shown here posing with a captured single-round, reloadable 122mm rocket-launcher unit designed and built for the NVA by the Soviet Union. The NVA labelled it the DKZ-B rocket artillery-launcher. (*USMC*)

Here a Marine provides a size comparison to a captured Soviet-designed and built 122mm rocket supplied to the NVA. The rocket was 6.2ft in length and weighed 121lb. The high-explosive warhead came in at 41lb. It took a crew of three to carry a DKZ-B rocket artillery-launcher unit. The range was approximately 12,000 yards. (*USMC*)

(**Opposite, above**) Seen here is a damaged Marine Corps' A-6 Intruder at the Da Nang air base after an NVA rocket attack. Besides the Soviet-supplied 122mm DKZ-B rocket artillery-launcher, the NVA was supplied with a Soviet 140mm rocket. It was 3.5ft in length, weighed 88lb and possessed a range of approximately 11,000 yards. (*USMC*)

(**Above**) Shown here lifting off with a stripped-down UH-34 helicopter is the massive Marine Corps' CH-37. The twin-engine helicopter had first entered service with the Marines in 1956. By the time of the Vietnam War, the piston-engine helicopter had become obsolete as more powerful gas-turbine-engine-powered helicopters replaced it in service. (*USMC*)

(**Opposite, below**) The replacement for the Marine Corps' piston-engine-powered UH-34s in South Vietnam would be the CH-46 Sea Knight helicopter, some of which are pictured here. The first examples arrived in the country in March 1966. Powered by two gas turbine engines, it in theory could carry up to seventeen passengers, not counting the three-man crew. (*USMC*)

(**Above**) Design problems with the original CH-46A Sea Knight helicopter that had caused loss of life in South Vietnam led to the introduction of the re-designed and improved 'D' model in 1967. The Sea Knight helicopter series had two 51ft-diameter rotors that overlapped each other at the centre of the aircraft's fuselage as pictured here. (*USMC*)

(**Opposite, above**) In the late 1950s, the Marine Corps decided that it needed a new gas-turbine-engine-powered helicopter to replace its piston-engine-powered OH-43D Huskies. In 1962, the decision was made to acquire a modified version of the US Army UH-1B Iroquois, better known by its unofficial nickname of the 'Huey'. The Marine Corps' Hueys received the designation UH-1E, with an example pictured here. (*USMC*)

(**Opposite, below**) The Marine Corps had at one point tried to come up with a gunship version of the UH-34 for use in South Vietnam. Unfortunately, the helicopter's design did not lend itself to that role. More successful in that role would be the Marine UH-1E. In this picture, the crew chief/door gunner of a UH-1E gunship is checking over its fixed forward-firing machine guns and 2.75in rocket pod. (*USMC*)

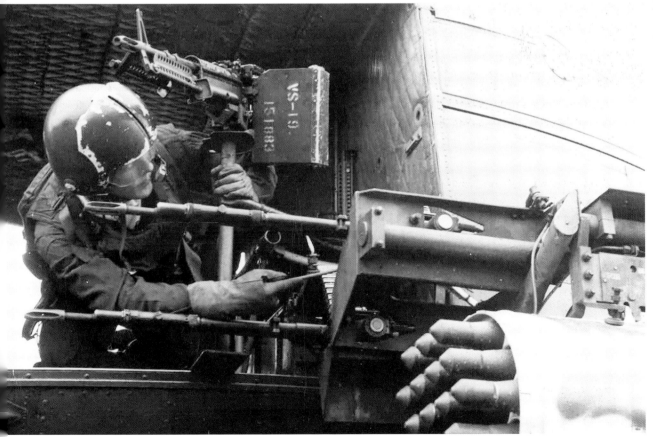

(**Above**) Posing for the photographer is a Marine sniper in South Vietnam armed with an M40 bolt-action sniper rifle. It had been adopted by the Marine Corps in great haste in 1966 and was essentially a slightly modified version of a commercial hunting rifle. Warping of the original walnut stock during the Vietnam War led to subsequent versions having fibreglass stocks. (*USMC*)

(**Opposite, above**) One of the more macabre practices of both the Marine Corps and US Army during the Vietnam War would be the so-called 'body count'. It was instituted by the American civilian Secretary of Defense Robert S. McNamara, who served from 1961 until 1968. He felt that only quantitative observations, such as enemy bodies, could provide a true picture of the measure of success in the Vietnam War. (*USMC*)

(**Opposite, below**) A tracked but unarmoured vehicle employed by the Marine Corps in South Vietnam would be the Amphibious Cargo Carrier M76 seen here and officially nicknamed the 'Otter'. The Marine Corps adopted it in the 1950s as the replacement for the Second World War-era M29 Weasel. During the Vietnam War, some crews attached thin sheet plates to the vehicle for a bit of protection. (*USMC*)

A Marine rifleman poses alongside an enemy defector who had volunteered to aid them in their fight against his former comrades. The enemy defectors were part of a Marine Corps' plan implemented in South Vietnam in 1966 referred to as the 'Kit Carson' programme. Such was its success that it would be adopted by the US Army the following year. (*USMC*)

The M60 machine gun pictured here, firing a 7.62mm round, would be the American military's replacement for the air-cooled .30 calibre Browning machine guns of the Second World War. The designers of the M60 incorporated elements of two German weapons of the Second World War into its design. Due to its weight and size, its unofficial nickname became the 'Pig'. (*USMC*)

A door gunner on a UH-34 is armed with an M60 machine gun and wears a lightweight fire-resistant flying overall. The helmet is a former pilot's headgear modified for use with the helicopter's internal intercom system. As helicopter door gunners proved very vulnerable to enemy small-arms ground fire during landing and take-offs, they often wore flak vests. (*USMC*)

Chapter Three

The Defining Year
(1968)

As had occurred in 1967, the Marine Corps' senior leadership found itself at odds with the MACV commander, General Westmoreland, on the conduct of the war. Like the enemy leadership, the Marines believed the path to victory lay with winning the hearts and minds of the South Vietnamese people. Westmoreland continued to feel that the quickest path to success involved the destruction of the military forces of the VC and NVA. In the end, Westmoreland's opinion prevailed.

At the same time, the Marines and Westmoreland engaged in debating the conduct of the war in 1968. There would be conflicting opinions on just what the New Year would hold for the Marines in I Corps. There were also rumours that the North Vietnamese government was interested in peace initiatives.

However, there were also reports of a growing enemy presence throughout I Corps. Adding to the confusion, the MACV's published intelligence estimates stated that enemy numbers had decreased; the opposite of what the US Central Intelligence Agency (CIA) reported.

Westmoreland remained upbeat, stating in early January 1968: 'The year [1967] ended with the enemy increasingly resorting to desperation tactics in attempting to achieve military/psychological victory; he has experienced only failure in these attempts … The friendly picture gives rise to optimism for increased successes in 1968.'

The Starting-Point
One point of contention between Marine leadership and Westmoreland at the start of 1968 centred on a small military base located in the far north-west corner of I Corps. Named Khe Sanh, the base bordered the neighbouring country of Laos. The NVA staged forces there, and had established major infiltration routes into South Vietnam. The enemy major infiltration routes into South Vietnam were collectively referred to as the 'Ho Chi Minh Trail'.

In October 1966, under pressure from Westmoreland, a Marine company occupied Khe Sanh. Previously a small team of US Army Special Forces soldiers and a

South Vietnamese militia unit occupied the site, beginning in 1962. The site also had a small airfield built by the French military in the 1950s. Following the Marines' arrival at Khe Sanh, the US Army soldiers and the South Vietnamese militiamen moved to a nearby location.

They're Here

On 24 April 1967, a Marine patrol operating outside the defensive perimeter of Khe Sanh engaged a large force of NVA troops, prompting the enemy's first attack on the base; that attack proved unsuccessful. In response, the Marines sent in reinforcements to seize some of the enemy-occupied hills circling the base. The operation lasted until May 1967, and is known as the 'Hill Battles'.

In June 1967, due to ever more enemy contacts, additional Marines were dispatched to Khe Sanh. There was now an entire Marine infantry battalion defending the base. Between August and early December of 1967, a lack of enemy contacts led to the transfer of some of the troops at the base to other roles.

As contact with enemy forces in the vicinity of Khe Sanh grew in mid-December 1967, a second Marine infantry battalion found itself committed to the base's defence. On 21 December 1967, a five-day sweep outside the base's perimeter revealed evidence of a growing enemy build-up. On 2 January 1968, MACV intelligence reports indicated the presence of two NVA divisions, and possibly a third, in the area around Khe Sanh.

On the evening of 2 January 1968, an alert Marine sentry spotted what appeared to be six Marines outside the concertina wire that surrounded Khe Sanh. When they failed to identify themselves, he opened fire, killing five and wounding the sixth, who managed to escape. The Marines examined the five corpses in Marine uniforms. Documents on their bodies showed them to be NVA senior regimental officers.

The Defenders

Following the 2 January incident, General Westmoreland ordered two additional Marine infantry battalions sent to Khe Sanh. The additional Marines brought the force defending the base to the size of a reinforced infantry regiment of approximately 6,000 men. To show his support, the senior ARVN general that operated within I Corps committed an understrength ARVN Ranger battalion to the base.

In addition to the five infantry battalions assigned to defend Khe Sanh, there were three batteries of 105mm howitzers and a single battery of 155mm howitzers and 4.2in mortars. Also assigned to its defence were a variety of armoured vehicles including five tanks. As a back-up for the protection of Khe Sanh, Westmoreland transferred to I Corps two US Army divisions, the initial elements of the first arriving on 19 January.

Let the Games Begin

An NVA junior officer captured on 20 January revealed an imminent major assault on Khe Sanh. The Marines on site went on high alert. That same day, the NVA mounted an attack on one of the Marine-held hills outside the base without seizing the position.

On 22 January, Khe Sanh came under heavy mortar, artillery and rocket attacks that destroyed its main ammunition dump. From a Marine Corps Historical Center publication comes this description of what then transpired:

> The dump erupted in a series of blinding explosions which rocked the base and belched thousands of artillery and mortar rounds into the air. Many of these maverick projectiles exploded on impact and added to the devastation.

Thousands of rounds were destroyed and much of this ammunition 'cooked off' in the flames for the next 48 hours. In addition, one enemy round hit a cache of tear gas [CS gas], releasing clouds of the pungent vapor which saturated the entire base.

Despite constant pounding by artillery for seventy-seven days, the NVA never mounted a significant attack on the Marines' defensive positions inside Khe Sanh's perimeter. However, they did attempt to capture some Marine-held locations outside the base but without success.

The only successful NVA breach of the Khe Sanh defensive perimeter occurred on 21 February, when the NVA launched a series of attacks against an understrength ARVN Ranger battalion holding a sector of the base's defensive lines. No doubt the NVA saw the ARVN unit as the weakest link in Khe Sanh's defences. However, even if the NVA attack had been successful, which it was not, the Marines had already established their own defensive lines behind the ARVN battalion.

The Khe Sanh Airlift

The aerial supply effort that supported Khe Sanh during its long siege did not come without cost. On 10 February a Marine C-130 bringing in fuel was just about to land when it was struck by enemy anti-aircraft fire. A description of what then occurred appears in an extract from a Marine Corps Historical Center publication: 'With flames licking at one side, the stricken craft careened off the runway 3,100 feet from the approach end, spun around, and was rocked by several muffled explosions. The C-130 then began to burn furiously. Crash crews rushed to the plane and starting spraying it with foam.'

Status Report on the NVA

The FMP/Pac staff had prepared a report in early January 1968 on the NVA's perceived strengths and weaknesses. The report began by listing it as 'one of the best in South-East Asia.' Recognizing the high morale of the NVA as a whole, the report stated that the typical soldier viewed '... the present conflict as one which has existed for two generations, and he has no great expectations that it will end soon, thus all of his actions are tempered by patience.'

On the negative side, the report listed the NVA's 'archaic logistical support system' and their '... inability to exploit any tactical opportunity calling for the rapid deployment of units and material.' The report also noted that after crossing the DMZ and experiencing the immense firepower that the Marines could inflict in battle, the typical NVA soldier's morale tended to deteriorate the longer he spent in action. That belief came from statements made by NVA prisoners of war.

The Dien Bien Phu Remake

With the NVA having cut the only land route to Khe Sanh in the autumn of 1967, the Marines at the base had to depend on aerial resupply. It was at this point that the resemblance to the successful Viet Minh two-month siege and eventual victory over the French garrison at Dien Bien Phu in 1954 began. In turn, this attracted the attention of both the American and foreign press. Hence, both American military and political prestige quickly became intertwined with keeping Khe Sanh from falling into enemy hands. American President Johnson became fixated on the base's day-to-day status.

The crash crews saved some of the flight crew and passengers, but six died in the crash. Thereafter landings by Marine C-130s were suspended. Instead, US Air Force C-130s received the assignment of bringing in supplies to Khe Sanh without landing on the base's airfield.

The US Air Force C-130s employed three different types of drop systems at Khe Sanh. One was referred to as the Low Altitude Parachute Extraction System (LAPES); another as the Ground Proximity Extraction System (GPES). However, due to the typically poor weather conditions around Khe Sanh, the majority of supplies were delivered by para-drops.

Bulk commodities, such as food rations and ammunition, were suitable for para-drop delivery but many other more fragile items such as medical supplies were not. US Air Force twin-engine, prop-driven C-123 Providers, along with Marine helicopters, therefore took on the job of landing and delivering these much-needed supplies. They also flew out the wounded and refugees trying to escape the fighting. Both the C-123s and helicopters took losses from these sorties.

The Battle for Khe Sanh Loses Steam

By mid-March, the Marines at Khe Sanh noticed an exodus of NVA units from the area. However, the NVA continued to maintain enough of their forces near the Marine base to still pose a threat. For example, on 23 March Khe Sanh was struck by 1,109 artillery rounds. However, with the reduction in enemy numbers, the base commander began pushing Marine and ARVN patrols ever further out from the defensive perimeter.

On 30 March a six-man Marine patrol discovered an entrenched NVA company on a small hill just outside the Khe Sanh defensive perimeter. Quickly driven off by heavy enemy fire, the Marine patrol called in supporting fire. A Marine company then assaulted the NVA position, in the aftermath dislodging the enemy from their bunkers with grenades, satchel charges and flame-throwers. A final count showed 115 NVA dead for the loss of 3 Marines killed and 15 wounded.

To the Rescue

As early as 26 January, General Westmoreland began formulating plans for a combined US Army and Marine relief force to break the NVA siege of Khe Sanh by both land and air assaults. Unfortunately, that plan had to be put off due to a large-scale enemy countrywide offensive operation that began on 30 January.

Relief of Khe Sanh was reconsidered on 28 February by the III MAF commander. When finalized, it received the name Operation PEGASUS and began on 1 April. On 6 April a US Army infantry unit arrived in Khe Sanh by helicopter as the relief force's leading element. On 8 April the first US Army ground unit reached the base, reopening the only land route to the area. That event marked Khe Sanh's official relief. Operation PEGASUS concluded on 15 April.

The MACV claimed without any real evidence that during the seventy-seven-day siege of Khe Sanh they accounted for some 10,000 to 15,000 enemy dead. Official North Vietnamese historical publications on the fighting around the base do not list their casualties. They do claim to have killed 13,000 American military personnel during the siege. The Marines stated that they had about 300 killed with approximately 2,500 wounded.

A Surprise Announcement

On 1 June, despite all the official statements made by various US Army and Marine generals (no doubt under duress) of the importance of keeping Khe Sanh open at all costs, the decision came to abandon it and much of the surrounding area to the NVA as it was a logistical and manpower drain on the III MAF.

US Army General Creighton Abrams replaced General Westmoreland on 11 June as directed by President Johnson. Westmoreland did not want the abandonment of Khe Sanh announced until he had left South Vietnam. It took until 5 July before the last Marine convoy departed the base after either destroying or salvaging whatever remained.

An interesting change occurred with Abrams' takeover of the MACV. Instead of Westmoreland's beloved search-and-destroy missions which were foisted on the III MAF, Abrams unveiled a new plan for populated areas that he referred to as 'clear and hold', which embraced what the Marines had been recommending since their arrival in South Vietnam. However, the American military never had enough ground forces in the area.

Who Held the Initiative?

Westmoreland had seen the threat posed to Khe Sanh as an essential first part in the NVA's attempt to outflank I Corps' two northernmost provinces. He believed that by holding the base at all costs, it would divert ever more of the enemy forces to the surrounding area. Once significant elements of the NVA had taken positions around

Khe Sanh, Westmoreland had planned to employ American airpower to destroy them, making it the decisive battle of the Vietnam War.

In his book *Khe Sanh 1967–1968: Marine Battles for Vietnam's Vital Hilltop Base*, published in 2005, Gordon L. Rottman suggested the two understrength NVA divisions (approximately 20,000 men including support troops) that surrounded Khe Sanh had the opposite goal: 'Was the [NVA] plan to actually overrun the base ... or was it merely to surround the base and draw and hold Free World forces there?'

A US Air Force historical monograph titled *Air Power and the Fight for Khe Sanh* published in 1973 observed that '... the North Vietnamese made no attempt to cut off Khe Sanh's water supply or to tunnel beneath the defensive works. Nor was there any evidence of an extensive network of siege trenches until the third week of February.'

Marine Brigadier General Lowell E. English, assistant division commander of the 3d Marine Division, had stated in 1967: 'When you're at Khe Sanh, you're not any place really ... You could lose it, and you wouldn't have lost a damn thing.' The South Vietnamese president at the time had expressed to Westmoreland his belief that Khe Sanh was only 'a diversionary effort' by the NVA.

Expected but Unprepared

On 30 January 1968, the enemy launched a well-coordinated, countrywide offensive operation on the cusp of the Vietnamese New Year holiday, hence the name 'Tet Offensive'. Involving almost 80,000 soldiers, NVA and Vietcong forces targeted the political infrastructure of the South Vietnamese government. ARVN and American military bases and the American Embassy in Saigon also came under attack.

American and ARVN intelligence services had had indications that the enemy might attack during Tet, but failed to grasp its massive scope. Westmoreland saw it as a feint to distract him from the siege of Khe Sanh and the battle for the control of the DMZ, which he believed remained the enemy's primary goals. It did not take long before Westmoreland's command staff at the MACV deduced it was the opposite.

American military leadership considered the Tet Offensive a severe tactical defeat; an opinion also held by the NVA due to extremely high losses. However, on a strategic level, the enemy succeeded in demoralizing the American public. Constantly reassured in print and broadcast on how well the war was going, the American public was rapidly disillusioned. Of interest is the fact that this had not been one of North Vietnam's goals. Instead, their primary target had been the demoralization of the South Vietnamese public.

Serious Indications Appear

Despite the fighting going at Khe Sanh in January 1968, the enemy remained active within other areas of I Corps during that same month, including another rocket attack on the Da Nang air base on the nights of 2 and 3 January. Those attacks accounted for three aircraft: one Marine and two US Air Force. By the end of the same month, enemy troop concentrations were detected by both Marine and US Army reconnaissance flights in areas surrounding the Da Nang air base.

Lieutenant Colonel Davis, commanding officer of the 1st Battalion, 7th Marines knew something big was going to happen on 27 January and explained why. '[We] … began to take fewer casualties from surprise firing devices [mines] or booby traps and began to suspect that enemy troops unfamiliar with the terrain might be attempting to move into this sector.' The Marine officer quickly notified his division headquarters.

Having killed a VC soldier on 29 January, a Marine patrol found documents on the corpse indicating what military targets would be of value to an attacking force in the Da Nang area. A very reliable Marine intelligence source stated that a massive enemy attack would begin no later than 30 January.

The Tet Offensive in I Corps

The Marines throughout the Da Nang area were on high alert when the Tet Offensive began within I Corps in the early-morning hours of 30 January. The enemy started with a massive rocket and mortar attack on the Da Nang air base, followed by two enemy assaults by small sapper units. Both penetrated its defensive perimeter, but were beaten off with the Marines taking minimal casualties.

One Marine would recall in a Marine Corps Historical Center publication his impressions of the fighting that broke out when trying to repel the constant enemy attacks: 'The sounds of the [artillery], the rockets, the mortars, the grenades combined with the eerie swaying of the illumination on their [flare] parachutes created a hellish vision. Never before or since have I been in such an acute state of fear.'

To counter the constant enemy attacks between 29 January and 14 February, the 1st Marines Division sent out several reconnaissance elements. One occupied a mountaintop position outside of the Da Nang air base, which spotted a large column of enemy soldiers estimated at 500 men. The immediate object of heavy artillery and aerial support, the enemy formation was hard hit.

A subsequent Marine intelligence report stated that an entire enemy battalion had been destroyed during a critical time during the Tet Offensive. The 1st Marine Division commander sent a message to III MAF headquarters in which he stated: 'Never have so few done so much to so many.'

What Happened?

In the opinion of both the Marines and the North Vietnamese, the various attacks against the Da Nang air base during the Tet Offensive proved poorly executed. In a captured enemy after-action report, the writer mentioned that his unit 'commander did not know … [the] situation accurately … and that orders were not strictly obeyed.' A Marine after-action report noted that the NVA 2nd Division's approach to Da Nang air base was 'along a single axis of advance so that his eventual target was easily identifiable.'

In the same Marine after-action report, the authors remained puzzled why the enemy, once arrived near the Da Nang air base, 'made no further attempts at maneuver even when being hunted by Marine and ARVN units, and when engaged, seldom maneuvered, except to withdraw'.

Some postulated that the Da Nang air base attack was carried out to divert attention from their planned attack on the undefended South Vietnamese city of Hue, also located within I Corps. At least one Marine general thought it was the other way around.

The Battle for Hue

When the enemy attacked Hue in the pre-dawn hours of 31 January, no Marine combat units were in the city. The closest units were located 7 miles outside of the city at the Phu Bai air base. These consisted of a Marine 1st Division support facility and a headquarters unit. The latter oversaw three understrength infantry battalions. The bulk of the division's assets had been assigned to guard the Da Nang air base as the III MAF perceived no threat to Hue.

An ARVN division had the responsibility for Hue's security. Unfortunately, its commander had also dismissed any idea that the enemy would mount an attack on the city. Hence, none of the ARVN division's infantry battalions were operating near the city. Only the division's headquarters resided within the city's limits, along with an MACV compound that housed the ARVN division's Marine, US Army and Australian advisers.

The enemy had massed three NVA regiments of about 5,000 men, a rocket battalion and a variety of local Vietcong units to capture Hue. The VC infiltrated the city under the cover of the vast throng of South Vietnamese civilians arriving to visit relatives during the upcoming holiday celebrations. The Vietcong were to prepare a path for the NVA regiments into the city limits. Before the sun rose on 31 January, the enemy had successfully occupied a great deal of Hue.

Clueless

With the attack on Da Nang air base in full swing and other enemy attacks reported throughout I Corps and beyond, the call from the MACV compound to the III MAF for help against the attack on Hue was not considered a pressing problem. The III MAP, therefore, ordered the Marine headquarters unit at Phu Bai to send an infantry company into Hue too. The Phu Bai air base itself came under enemy rocket and mortar fire on 31 January.

On entering the Hue city limits, the Marine infantry company, along with four medium tanks picked up along the way, ran into a wall of enemy fire. A second Marine infantry company, sent in response to the first company's calls for help, quickly found itself also pinned down by enemy fire. The Marine leadership of the III MAP still had no idea of the massive scale of the enemy's attack on the city.

It took numerous reports from Marines fighting for their lives for the III MAP Marine leadership to realize the seriousness of what had taken place in the city. A Marine general commented in a Marine Corps Historical Center publication: 'Early intelligence did not reveal the quantity of enemy involved that we subsequently found were committed to Hue.' Finally, on 1 February, both Marine and ARVN senior leadership grasped what had happened in Hue and sent in sufficient forces to retake those parts of the city in enemy hands.

The Fighting Heats Up

The Marines eventually committed three infantry battalions to recapturing their assigned portion of Hue. In contrast, the AVRN put fifteen infantry battalions into the fight for the city. It was a matter of national pride for the South Vietnamese government that they play the major part in retaking Hue. US Army units also contributed to the fighting around Hue but did not reach the city until 25 February.

A Marine captain in Hue observed: 'Street-fighting is the dirtiest type of fighting I know.' A Marine fire team leader agreed, 'it's tougher in the streets' but also went on to remark, 'it beats fighting in the mud … You don't get tired as quickly when you are running, and you can see more of the damage you're doing to the enemy because they don't drag off their dead.'

The Marine infantry battalions had support from lightly-armoured Ontos fighting vehicles, armed with six 106mm recoilless rifles. The 1st Marine regimental commander commented that during the battle 'if any single supporting arm is to be more effective than all others, it must be the 106mm recoilless rifle, especially on the Ontos.' Hard, vicious fighting in Hue demanded innovative solutions:

> Unable to position their [recoilless rifle] to knock out a machine gun that blocked the battalion's advance, [its crew] took their 460-pound recoilless rifle [inside a building] … and we fired it with a lanyard where we knocked out the objective – we kind of knocked out the building that the 106 was in too, but it didn't hurt the gun, once we dug it out.

Lieutenant Colonel Ernest C. Cheatham Jr commented on the use of tanks in the recapture of Hue: 'You couldn't put a section of tanks down one of those streets. The moment a tank stuck its nose around the corner of a building it looked like the Fourth of July.' The tanks themselves soon became known as 'rocket magnets' due to the enemy's widespread use of anti-tank rocket-propelled grenade (RPG)-launchers.

Just About Finished

By 6 February a Marine lieutenant colonel in Hue noticed the enemy's resistance to his battalion's advance slacking and later commented: 'He [the NVA] seemed to lose his stomach for the fight … once we started rolling … the main force sort of evaporated … and left some local force – rinky dinks … when his defense crumbled, it crumbled.' By the next day, as the Marine infantry battalions advanced further into what had been the NVA defensive positions, they found both bodies and equipment left behind.

The ARVN declared Hue secure on 26 February, even though scattered fighting in and around the city would continue for another three weeks. The Marines had announced the city secure the day before. However, it took until 5 March before Operation HUE CITY officially came to an end. The Marines claimed they accounted for almost 2,000 enemy killed during the fighting.

Marine losses during Operation HUE CITY came in at 142 dead and approximately 1,005 wounded. A Marine rifleman commented on an issue that bothered him: '… the stink – you had to load up so many wounded, the blood would dry on your hands. In two or three days you would smell like death itself.'

The Enemy keeps up the Pressure

Beginning in April, the 3d Marine Division became aware of an enemy build-up by an NVA division in the eastern portion of the DMZ. This posed a threat to the Marines' main logistical base at the port of Dong Ha. The Marines therefore brought in both infantry and supporting tanks. The fiercest fighting, which began on 29 April, developed at a village not too far from Dong Ha, named Dai Do, that the enemy had managed to slip into without notice and had quickly fortified.

As the ARVN proved unable to take the village of Dai Do or prevent other enemy actions aimed at Dong Ha, Marines from the 3d Marine Division responded. In trying to oust the enemy from Dai Do, a Marine lieutenant remembered: 'The enemy counter-attack dwarfed the fighting that had gone before in intensity and volume.

The Tet Series

The initial Tet Offensive ran from 30 January until 28 March. The second in the same series took place between 5 May and 15 June and received the name 'Mini-Tet'. The final enemy offensive of the year and considered part of the Tet series began on 17 August and continued until 23 September. It would be referred to by the American military by several different names, including the 'Phase III Offensive', 'The Third Offensive' or 'The Autumn Offensive'. However, the second and third in the series of Tet Offensive operations did not come close to matching the scale of the first.

I recall seeing banana trees and the masonry wall of a hooch cut down by the [NVA] automatic weapon fire. The bushes to our front seemed to be alive with heavily camouflaged NVA soldiers.'

By the time the fighting at Dai Do ended on 3 May, the Marines had suffered 81 dead and about 300 wounded. However, the battle was not over, as the NVA division continued to press the attack until the end of May in the general area of Dong Ha until all were eventually repulsed. From a Marine Corps Historical Center publication appears the following passage:

In many respects, questions still remain about the intent of the enemy. Obviously, the thrust of the 320th [enemy division] was part of the overall NVA so-called 'mini-Tet offensive' that the enemy attempted in May to initiate country-wide, a somewhat 'poor man's imitation' of the January-February Tet offensive.

A New Sheriff in Town

On 20 May 1968, Major General Raymond G. Davis became commander of the 3d Marine Division. A Second World War veteran and Korean War Medal of Honor winner, General Davis had some firm ideas on how his division could improve its combat capabilities. The first would be restoration of unit integrity, meaning there would be no more mixing and matching of infantry battalions and infantry companies between infantry regiments under normal operating conditions.

Second, General Davis had been very impressed by the US Army's 1st Airmobile Division use of its large inventory of helicopters to move quickly over the varied terrain of South Vietnam and at the same time keep the enemy off-balance.

General Davis's desire to emulate the US Army's new airmobile division abilities came at an opportune moment. At the time he took command the Marine Corps had finally acquired enough helicopters of sufficient lifting power to match that of the US Army in the theatre.

With the new fleet of helicopters, General Davis could shift his troops from the much-despised defensive posture forced on them by such situations as Khe Sanh and take the offensive to the enemy. So, beginning in the summer of 1968, the Marines of the 3d Division began fanning out across the northernmost province of I Corps. Thus, they attacked the enemy in what were long considered safe havens. By the end of the year, the NVA could no longer deal with the fast-moving Marines and withdrew the bulk of their forces back across the DMZ or into their sanctuaries in Laos.

Da Nang Again in the Crosshairs

In the central province of I Corps, the Da Nang air base and large civilian population remained a key enemy target. Even as the Marines of the 1st Division prepared for

Fire Support Bases

An essential aspect of the success of the 3d Marine Division's new-found enhanced mobility would be another tactical innovation referred to as Fire Support Bases (FSBs). From a Marine Corps Historical Center publication is the following explanation of the concept of an FSB: 'A rapidly constructed artillery position defended by a minimum of infantry. The infantry and tactical elements within the protective fan of the artillery FSB. The FSB themselves offer overlapping artillery support to each other and protection for several landing zones.'

The concept of FSBs would allow the Marines of the 3d Division to operate throughout their zone of operation with constant protective fire from artillery. By the end of 1968, the 3d Marine Division had carved out more than 140 temporary FSBs from jungle mountain hilltops. So successful did the concept of FSBs become that it would soon be employed throughout South Vietnam.

their next offensive operation, the enemy would be doing the same. The Marines beat them to it with Operation ALLEN BROOK that began on 4 May. It badly disrupted a large NVA assault planned for 5 May on the Da Nang air base as part of mini-Tet.

In spite of not mounting a ground attack on Da Nang air base in May, the tempo of enemy rocket attacks did increase. In conjunction with Operation ALLEN BROOK, the Marines of the 1st Division began another operation named MAMELUKE THRUST that, like the former, acted as spoiling attacks on areas near the Da Nang air base that might harbour NVA concentrating sites.

In a Marine Corps Historical Center publication, a Marine corporal who had taken part in Operation MAMELUKE THRUST recalled finding himself at a Hospital Company after being wounded several times. When a doctor enquired what was wrong with him:

> I said, 'Well, I got stabbed in the back, I got bit in the arm, I got shrapnel in the chest, and I got shot in the leg.' He couldn't believe it until he looked at it. He thought it was kinda funny. I wasn't in a mood to laugh at it.

Operation MAMELUKE THRUST ran from 19 to 24 May, while Operation ALLEN BROOK continued until 24 August as by that time the enemy had withdrawn. The latter would return to the area in increasing numbers in early September to prepare for their final Tet series offensive operation against the Da Nang air base and the city of Da Nang.

The Marines concluded that the third and last major attack on the Da Nang air base would begin on 23 August, which it did. The NVA's and VC's spirited assaults were, as so often before, beaten off with high losses. By 31 August the final Tet series offensive had spent itself. In the weeks that followed, running into September, the Marines conducted only mopping-up operations.

With the advent of the north-east monsoon rains in October, both sides decreased their activities for the remainder of the year. Rather than large-scale offensive operations, the enemy turned to small-scale assaults on weakly-defended targets, as well as rocket and mortar attacks on both military and civilian targets.

Looking Back Over the Year

Some significant events took place outside of South Vietnam in 1968 that would influence the Marine Corps' further participation in the Vietnam War. The first occurred on 13 May when American and South Vietnamese government representatives sat down in Paris, France with their North Vietnamese counterparts. The purpose was to seek a peace agreement to bring an end to the fighting. The peace talks quickly broke down, but were restarted on 1 November.

On 5 November, Richard M. Nixon, who had campaigned on the promise to end the Vietnam War with 'peace and honor', was elected president of the United States. He took office in January 1969. In December the number of enemy-initiated attacks had fallen to the lowest level over the previous two years. At the end of December, the III MAF claimed to have accounted for 31,691 enemy dead. The cost to the Marines came to 4,618 dead and 29,320 wounded, making it the costliest year of the Vietnam War for the Marine Corps.

At the beginning of 1968, the typical Marine had to deal with endless rain brought on by the yearly monsoon in South-East Asia that made his life miserable. Little did he care that the enemy had suffered endless defeats since America's large-scale military intervention had begun in 1965. By the beginning of 1968, estimates of the enemy losses came in at approximately 88,000 men since 1965. (USMC)

Marines are shown here dealing with the rain and wishing they were back home. By the beginning of 1968, there had appeared a degree of inter-service dissent between the US forces. The senior US Army officers at the MACV believed that the Marines under the III MAF were not pulling their full weight in the conflict. *(USMC)*

In this photograph we see four-star General Robert E. Cushman as commandant of the Marine Corps. As a three-star lieutenant general, he had commanded the III MAF throughout 1968. With his headquarters located at the Da Nang air base, his authority had extended 220 miles from the Demilitarized Zone (DMZ) in the north to the southern border with II Corps overseen by the US Army. *(USMC)*

Pictured here is a US Army M107 175mm self-propelled gun at one of the Marine Corps' bases used to provide long-range fire support to the KSCB in 1967 and 1968. From the muzzle of the gun to the rear of its firing mechanism it had a length of almost 36ft. It fired an HE round weighing 147lb out to a maximum range of 25 miles (44,000 yards), making it the longest-range artillery piece employed during the Vietnam War. (USMC)

Beginning in April 1967 through to May 1967 the III MAF set about seizing the hills around the KSCB to prevent the NVA using them to emplace their artillery. The fighting that involved these terrain features became known as the 'Hill Battles' and were company- and battalion-sized actions. Marine losses during the Hill Battles came in at 155 killed and 425 wounded. (USMC)

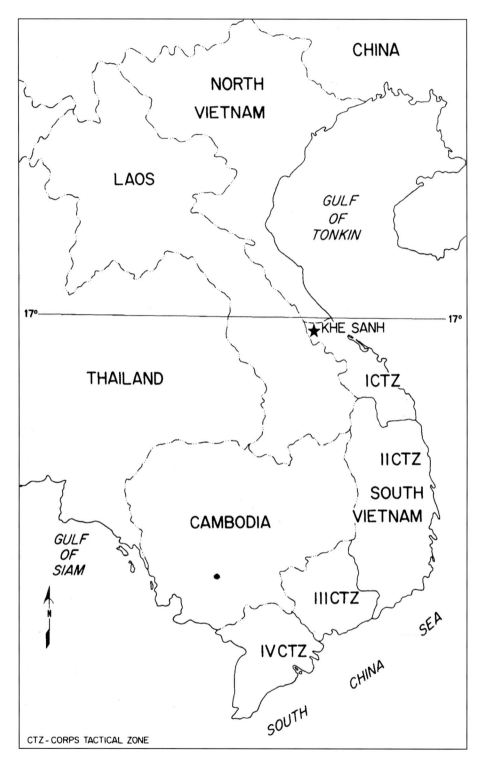

The continuing infiltration of large NVA units down the Ho Chi Minh trail through Laos and into South Vietnam in 1967 proved to be a major concern to Westmoreland. To interdict the NVA he ordered the III MAF to increase its force levels at the Khe Sanh Combat Base (KSCB) and the surrounding area. As seen on this map, the KSCB was located at the extreme north-western corner of South Vietnam. (*USMC*)

The physical strain of patrolling in the jungles of South Vietnam with their heat and humidity is seen on the face of the Marine rifleman pictured here. There is a radio on his back and the handset attached to his shoulder. The FM radio's designation would have been the AN/PRC-10. Considered unreliable, its eventual replacement would be the AN/PRC-25. (*USMC*)

A pair of F-4B Phantom IIs of Marine Fighter Attack Squadron-542 (VMFA-542), officially nicknamed the 'Bengals', are on a mission over South Vietnam in January 1969. The squadron first arrived at the Da Nang air base in July 1965. It remained in South Vietnam until January 1970. The letter prefix 'V' in the squadron's designation is an old US Navy label for 'heavier-than-air'. (*USMC*)

The M14 rifles in the hands of the Marine riflemen pictured here possibly date the photograph to before late 1967, the point at which the Marines began switching to the M16 rifle. The Marine in the foreground, and presumably the others, are wearing the M1955 Armor-Body Fragmentation Protective, known to all as a 'flak vest'. (*USMC*)

Employed by the Marine Corps during the Vietnam War would be the Carrier, Cargo, Amphibious M116 1.5-ton vehicle best known by its official nickname of the 'Husky'. The non-armoured aluminium vehicle weighed 10,600lb and was fully amphibious, using its tracks for propulsion in the water. Top speed in the water was 4.2mph and on land 37mph. (*USMC*)

A Marine Corps M114A1 155mm towed howitzer is pictured here during a fire mission in South Vietnam. It weighed more than 6 tons (12,000lb) and was serviced by a detachment of eleven men. Classified as medium artillery, it was intended for engaging enemy artillery, dug-in enemy personnel and soft-skin (non-armoured) vehicles. *(USMC)*

Pictured here at the Da Nang air base in South Vietnam is an A-4 Skyhawk. A-4s first entered into squadron service with the Marine Corps in 1957. Prior to US military involvement in the Vietnam War there were twelve front-line Marine squadrons equipped with the aircraft. The standard version employed would be labelled the 'E' model. *(USMC)*

Taking off from the US Navy's USS *Princeton* (LPH-5) in March 1966, just off the coast of South Vietnam, are Marine Corps UH-34D troop transport helicopters. The piston-engine-powered helicopter had first entered into Marine Corps' service in 1957 and initially became operational in South Vietnam in 1962 to aid the ARVN. Its popular nickname was the 'HUS'. (*US Navy*)

A young Marine officer holds a captured enemy AKM assault rifle which is missing its standard thirty-round curved magazine. The enemy was supplied with both the original AK-47 with a milled steel receiver and the later improved AKM with a stamped steel receiver. The AKM pictured here does not have the spiked bayonet normally seen on Chinese-made copies. (*USMC*)

A preserved example of a Marine Corps Landing Vehicle Tracked, Passenger (LVTP-5A1) as was employed during the Vietnam War. The driver's position was on the front left-hand side and the vehicle commander's on the front right-hand side. Entry and egress from the vehicle would be via the large hydraulically-operated ramp at the front. The gasoline engine was located at the rear of the vehicle. *(Paul and Loren Hannah)*

Marines manning an M60 machine gun on the defence in South Vietnam. The weapon shown here is mounted on an M91 tripod. When the barrel on the M60 needed to be replaced it required the use of an asbestos mitten as it would be too hot to touch. The loss of the mitten could make changing a barrel very difficult in the field. *(USMC)*

Pictured here is a Marine Corps M48A3 medium tank armed with a 90mm main gun. For improved visibility it has been fitted with a G305 turret riser located below the tank commander's cupola and above the turret roof. Not seen here is the .50 calibre machine gun that normally armed the tank commander's cupola. The device over the rear of the barrel is an infrared searchlight. *(USMC)*

In this artist's interpretation we see a mine or booby trap going off among Marines in a patrol during the Vietnam War. From an American government publication on the Viet Cong released during the Vietnam War appears this passage: 'Homemade booby traps, ranging from simple deadfalls and spike-boards to explosive foot-mines are often used in preparing for a battle or an ambush.' *(USMC)*

Two Marine infantrymen are seen here during the battle for the South Vietnamese city of Hue in January/February 1968. Both are armed with M16 rifles that fired a 5.56mm round. Some Marine units during the fighting swapped their M16 rifles for the older-generation M14 rifles as they fired a more powerful 7.62mm round better suited to urban combat. (*USMC*)

Urban combat typically entailed heavy casualties for the attackers, and the Battle for Hue was no different for the Marine units that took part in retaking the city. Pictured here are Marine infantrymen huddled behind a wall for cover from enemy fire. One Marine helps to bandage another, with a Marine in the background talking on a radio hand-set. (*USMC*)

Pictured here is an unrestored example of a 155mm self-propelled gun M53 employed by the Marine Corps during the Vietnam War. The weapon-armed turret has limited right and left transverse, unlike the later-generation 155mm self-propelled howitzer M109. There was storage for twenty rounds on board the M53. *(Chris Hughes)*

Here taking part in an air show is a restored OV-10A Bronco in Marine Corps markings. The twin turbo-prop aircraft had a crew of two and began service with the Marine Corps in South Vietnam in 1968. It replaced the O-1 Bird Dog, not only in the artillery observation role but also as a Forward Air Controller (FAC). *(Christophe Vallier)*

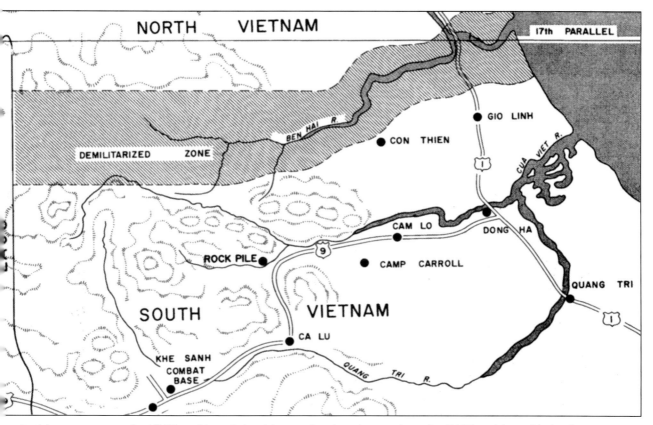

In this map, we see the KSCB and its relationship to other locations such as the DMZ and Laos. Marine bases at 'Camp Carroll' and the 'Rock Pile' had US Army M107 175mm self-propelled guns. These weapons were employed to dominate the surrounding area including the KSCB. Route 9 was a one-lane dirt road and the only supply line to the KSCB and was routinely cut by the NVA. (*USMC*)

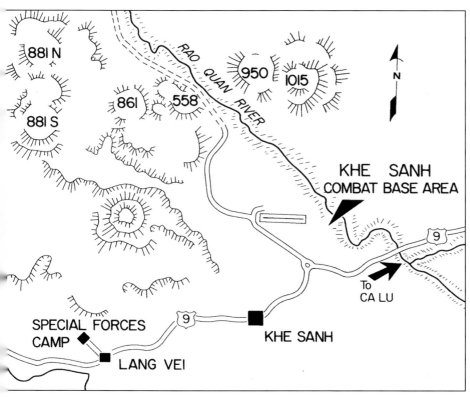

In this map, we see the location of the KSCB and its relationship to Highway 9 and the small village of Khe Sanh seized by the NVA on 21 January 1968. Also identified is the US Army Lang Vei Special Forces Camp that fell to the NVA on 7 February 1968. The KSCB existed on a small triangular plateau dominated by large hills that formed part of a mountain range named the Annamites in Laos. (*USMC*)

(**Opposite, above**) With Westmoreland's continued insistence on the strengthening and enlargement of the KSCB, the Marine units assigned began the process of heavily fortifying the base. The first step would be making sandbags as pictured here. In December 1967, the Marines became aware that instead of passing down the Ho Chi Minh Trail near the KSCB the NVA units were staying in the area. (*USMC*)

(**Above**) A picture of the sandbagged defensive positions along the western perimeter of the KSCB in early 1968. Fortification material proved to be in short supply as the trees in the surrounding area had metal fragments embedded in them from artillery and air strikes and could not be cut. The Marine positions around the KSCB consisted of mutually-supported strongpoints. (*USMC*)

(**Opposite, below**) Typical of the fighting bunkers erected by the Marines at the KSCB at the beginning of 1968 is the example pictured here. Note the firing port. After a visit by the III MAP commander to the KSCB, he ordered that all bunkers had enough overhead cover capable of withstanding a direct hit by an 82mm mortar round. To strengthen their bunkers, the Marines used damaged portions of the airstrip's steel matting. (*USMC*)

Marines are shown here erecting a concertina razor wire entanglement around the KSCB. Because razor wire is relatively lightweight and inexpensive, it can go up quickly. Easily breached by enemy artillery fire, it is rapidly repairable. To deter enemy engineers (sappers) from breaching the concertina razor wire entanglements surrounding the KSCB, the Marines booby-trapped them. (*USMC*)

For the defence of the KSCB, there were eighteen 105mm towed howitzers with an example pictured here. Fifteen were emplaced within the combat base with three others positioned on one of the Marine-occupied hills surrounding the KSCB. There were also six of the 4.2in (107mm) mortars assigned to defend the KSCB as well as towed 155mm howitzers. (*USMC*)

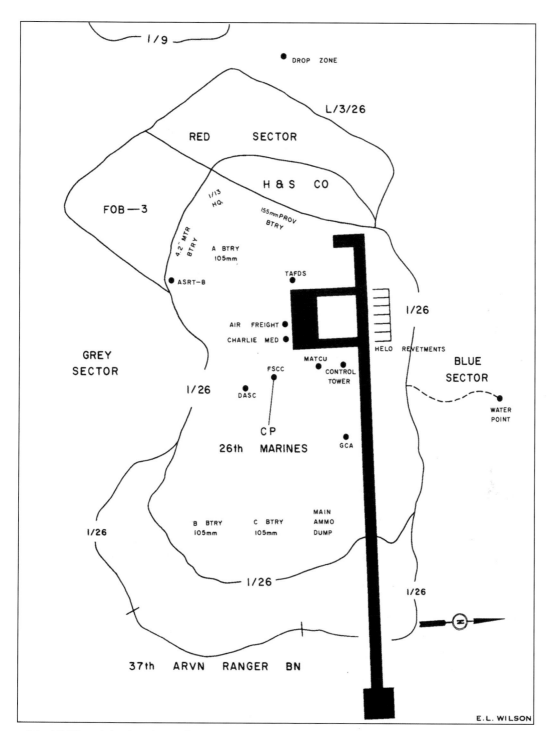

A map of the KSCB and the locations of the defending units with the airfield outlined in black. The Marines in some places around the combat base emplaced metal drums containing a mixture of gasoline and diesel fuel. When and if the NVA attacked, the Marines would set off the fuel-filled drums with plastic explosives, creating a wall of flame that would no doubt discourage the most determined attackers. (USMC)

(**Opposite, above**) Also contributing to the defence of the KSCB in 1968 were 106mm recoilless rifles as pictured here. Their accuracy was such that they could hit pinpoint targets, including something as small as a single enemy sniper. Besides anti-tank and HE rounds, the weapon could fire the XM546 Beehive round that contained 8,000 arrow-like flechettes. (*USMC*)

(**Opposite, below**) Here a Marine is aiming with the optical sighting scope on his 106mm recoilless rifle. When a target is acquired, he pulls a trigger that fires a special .50 calibre phosphorus tracer round from a single-shot barrel bolted to the 106mm recoilless rifle. The .50 calibre round has the same trajectory as the 106mm recoilless round and if on target the gunner fires the larger round. (*USMC*)

(**Above**) To strengthen the defences at the KSCB, the US Army supplied two of its twin 40mm self-propelled gun M42A1s; a preserved example is pictured here. Each of its two 40mm automatic cannons could fire 120 rounds per minute (rpm) for a combined total of 240 rpm. Also the US Army contributed two unarmoured trucks each armed with a quad .50 calibre M55 armour-protected powered mount. (*Pierre-Olivier Buan*)

At the beginning of 1968, the 1st MAW consisted of 15,000 men and 400 aircraft in South Vietnam. Of that number, approximately half were fixed-wing aircraft such as the A-4 Skyhawks pictured here, and the other half helicopters. Continuing problems for the 1st MAW during the Vietnam War were both a shortage of pilots and mechanics with the necessary skills to maintain the aircraft. (USMC)

A Marine pilot of an A-4 Skyhawk examines a hole made in the wing of his aircraft by an NVA anti-aircraft gun while flying in support of the KSCB. Due to the thick foliage covering the terrain around the combat base and poor flying conditions, plus night-time aerial strikes, it proved very difficult for Marine aviation and the USAF to properly assess the effectiveness of their sorties. (USMC)

A relatively unknown fixed-wing aircraft in the Marine Corps inventory during the Vietnam War was the KC-130 four-engine transport pictured here configured for the air-to-air refuelling role. They also were employed to fly supplies and reinforcements throughout the Western Pacific. They played an important part in the re-supply of the KSCB. (*USMC*)

The NVA began a massive artillery, rocket and mortar attack on the KSCB on 21 January 1968. The enemy would continue to shell the combat base during the entire seventy-seven-day siege. This forced the Marines on site to spend a great deal of their time under some cover, as are those pictured here. The Marines estimated that the NVA fired approximately 11,000 rounds into the KSCB and surrounding positions. (*USMC*)

Among the many weapons with which the NVA bombarded the KSCB was the Soviet-designed and built Model 1938 120mm mortar. Placed into Red Army service during the Second World War, it fired a 35lb HE round out to a maximum range of approximately 4 miles (7,040 yards). Due to its size and weight, it was a towed weapon. *(Vladimir Yakubov)*

A modern artillery piece supplied to the NVA during the Vietnam War and employed against the KSCB was the 152mm gun/howitzer M1955 pictured here. It was also designated the D-20 and weighs approximately 12,500lb. Developed during the late 1940s it was first seen in Soviet Army service in 1955. The maximum firing range was 11 miles (19,360 yards). *(Pierre-Olivier Buan)*

The second longest-range artillery piece employed by any combatant during the Vietnam War would be the 130mm field gun M1954 pictured here. A Soviet-designed and built artillery piece from the 1950s, it weighed in at 17,000lb and had a maximum range of 17 miles (29,920 yards). The extremely long barrel seen in this picture was 22ft 2in in length. *(Pierre-Olivier Buan)*

Among the Marine Corps' helicopters that flew in supplies to the KSCB during the siege is the gas-turbine-engine-powered CH-53 series seen here. The original 'A' version first arrived in South Vietnam in December 1966. Among the other roles it assumed, it replaced the CH-37 for recovery of downed helicopters. *(USMC)*

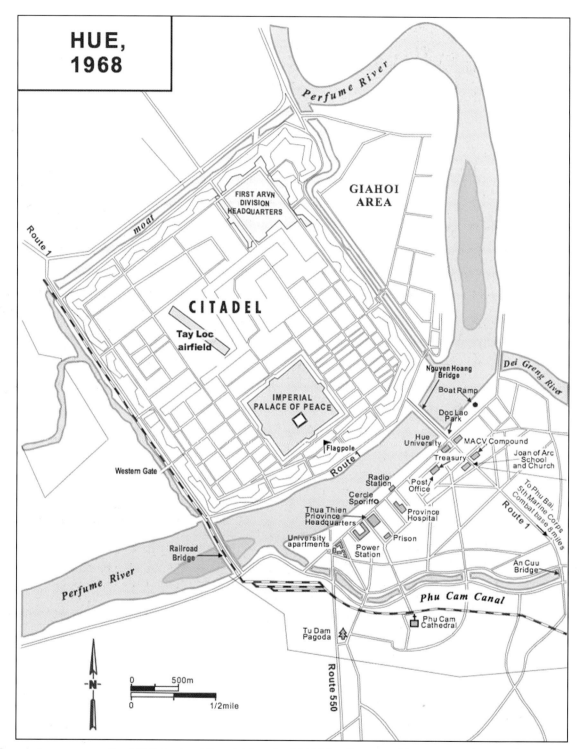

HUE, 1968

Perfume River

GIAHOI AREA

Route 1

moat

FIRST ARVN DIVISION HEADQUARTERS

CITADEL

Tay Loc airfield

IMPERIAL PALACE OF PEACE

Flagpole

Route 1

Western Gate

Nguyen Hoang Bridge

Boat Ramp

Doc Lao Park

Hue University

MACV Compound

Treasury

Joan of Arc School and Church

Dei Greng River

Radio Station

Post Office

Cercle Sporiff

Province Hospital

Thua Thien Priovince Headquarters

University apartments

Power Station

Prison

Railroad Bridge

To Phu Bai, 5th Marine Corps Combat base 8 miles

Route 1

An Cuu Bridge

Perfume River

Phu Cam Canal

Phu Cam Cathedral

Tu Dam Pagoda

Route 550

-N-

0 500m

0 1/2mile

For whatever reasons the ARVN had not thought that the NVA/Viet Cong would mount a major assault on Hue, the former Imperial Capital of Vietnam. That proved erroneous and as part of the countrywide Tet Offensive, beginning on 31 January 1968, enemy forces took control of most of the city with little ARVN resistance. The map shown here illustrates the various key locations in the city. *(US Army)*

An all-too-common event during the Vietnam War would be the ceremony seen here, honouring those Marines who died in the service of their country. By the time the seventy-seven-day siege of the KSCB officially lifted on 8 April 1968, the Marines had taken approximately 300 killed with 2,500 wounded. NVA losses were estimated between 10,000 to 15,000 men. (*USMC*)

In an official Marine Corps photo taken in Hue, following the enemy capture of the city, is a knocked-out ARVN M41 light tank. The ARVN committed eleven battalions of troops to the recapture of the city. As Hue fell within the III MAP area of responsibility, three Marine infantry battalions were committed to capturing a portion of the city. Four US Army infantry battalions would also take part. (*USMC*)

(**Above**) The first two Marine infantry companies sent to Hue encountered extremely stiff enemy resistance. On that first day, the Marines lost ten men killed and fifty-six wounded. Pictured here are Marines in Hue, carefully checking out their surroundings. One of the two has a radio with the antenna folding downward. (*USMC*)

(**Opposite, above**) On 1 February 1968, the Marines once again pushed into Hue with two companies supported by a tank. That attack quickly came to a halt when an enemy recoilless rifle knocked out the supporting tank. At that point, there remained little information on just how large a force the Marines were facing. Marine infantrymen in Hue are hugging a wall for protection from enemy fire. (*USMC*)

(**Opposite, below**) A Marine armed with an M60 machine gun is seen engaging the enemy during the Battle for Hue. The fighting in the city started with the Marines trying to secure individual buildings. However, the enemy was so determined to hold their positions that the fighting quickly reverted to room-to-room combat. (*USMC*)

(**Opposite, above**) A Marine Corps' sniper takes part in the Battle for Hue. In a US Army manual on urban combat appears this extract on the importance of snipers: 'In open terrain, snipers slightly influence operations. In UO [urban operations], snipers – well-concealed, positioned and protected – can take on significance disproportionate to their combat capability in other situations.' (*USMC*)

(**Above**) Besides using explosive charges to bore through the walls of enemy-held buildings, the Marines also employed 3.5in rocket-launchers to blast holes through courtyard and building walls. Another building-busting weapon would be the 106mm recoilless rifle seen here being humped by a group of Marines. (*USMC*)

(**Opposite, below**) If a single 106mm recoilless rifle could be effective in the urban combat that took place in Hue, then six firing at one time had to be even better. The first Multiple 106mm Self-Propelled Rifle M50A1 vehicles, known as the 'Ontos', reached Hue on 2 February 1968. Despite being only thinly-armoured and having to be reloaded from the outside, they were highly thought of by the Marines fighting in Hue. (*USMC*)

A Marine M60 machine-gun team in action in Hue. Offensive urban operations are considered to be one of the most challenging operations that an infantry force can undertake. The density of urban structures can require the attacking force to have three to five times greater personnel density than for a similar mission conducted in open terrain. (*USMC*)

Marines in Hue are seen here evacuating a wounded comrade. By its very nature, urban combat can result in increased casualties. From a US Army manual on urban combat appears this passage: 'The urban terrain provides numerous advantages to the urban defender; higher casualties occur among troops on the offensive, where frontal assaults may be the only tactical options.' (*USMC*)

Here a Marine is employing his 40mm M79 single-shot grenade-launcher to engage the enemy in a building in Hue with high-angle fire. Urban combat can be very time-consuming due to the need for initial reconnaissance of the objective(s) and the physical and mental stress it can impose on the attackers. Having to deal with the needs of the urban population can also hinder operational timelines. (*USMC*)

A Marine rifleman fighting in Hue has adopted for use a Second World War Submachine Gun, Calibre .45 M1, best known to most by its unofficial nickname as the 'Tommy Gun' or 'Thompson'. One can assume that it's a captured Viet Cong weapon as the NVA soldiers typically had more modern small arms. It could have also been a left-behind South Vietnamese police weapon. (*USMC*)

An M67A1 flame-thrower tank in Hue. It can be identified by the thicker and shorter barrel than seen on the M48A3 medium tanks armed with a 90mm main gun. An important task in urban combat is to separate the local civilian population from combatants. Field commanders must also do their best to minimize collateral damage if at all possible. (USMC)

In urban combat, the enemy often has the advantage of interior lines. The defending enemy can reinforce or reposition their units using concealed routes such as sewer systems. Such transit routes can allow the defending enemy to appear behind the attacking force's front lines. This calls for the attackers to maintain stay-behind forces to deal with such a threat. (USMC)

An enemy soldier who fell in combat during the Battle for Hue. For the attackers in urban combat environments the corpses of the dead, be it the enemy or the local civilians, can quickly pose a serious health risk to all concerned. That and the breakdown of the local sewer systems only adds to the complexities of urban combat. *(USMC)*

Field commanders in urban combat situations have to deal with the often heavy logistical demands of their personnel in the front lines. Ideally, the supporting elements are closely following the attacking force. The weak links are the roads and bridges that lead back to the logistical supply bases. Pictured here is a bridge in Hue destroyed by the enemy. *(USMC)*

Another favourite weapon among the Marines fighting in Hue was their 81mm mortar, as shown here during the fighting. One Marine officer commented that 'If you put enough 81 rounds on top of a building, pretty soon the roof falls in.' He then went on to state that the orders from his commanding officer were 'if we even suspected that the enemy were in a building to blow it down.' *(USMC)*

A Marine officer wrote on 5 February 1968 that he lacked enough men to perform the jobs assigned in Hue. He also went on to state that it was 'an extremely rough day' with the battalion sustaining nineteen casualties and advancing only 75 yards. He remembered: 'The going was slow. We would go at maybe a block. We fought for two days over one building.' *(USMC)*

(**Above**) A picture of an M48A3 medium tank during the Battle for Hue. The Marine riflemen welcomed tank firepower in Hue. The downside of tank support going back to the Second World War for Marine riflemen is that they tend to attract a lot of fire due to the threat they pose to the enemy. They have been referred to by many in the field as 'bullet or artillery magnets'. (*USMC*)

(**Opposite, above**) The Marine Corps M48A3 tank pictured here during the Battle for Hue sports a spacer ring under the original machine-gun-armed cupola equipped with nine large periscopes. Its purpose was to improve the tank commander's vision without having to expose his head or upper torso out of the top of his cupola. Vehicles so equipped were referred to as the M48A3 (Mod B) tanks. (*USMC*)

(**Opposite, below**) Marine replacements are seen here heading to Hue. It took until 2 March 1968 before the Battle for Hue was officially over. Marine losses in the fighting came in at 142 dead and 1,100 wounded. Total allied casualties, including US Army units and South Vietnamese military forces, were approximately 600 dead with 3,800 wounded. (*USMC*)

(**Above**) Seen here in South Vietnam is a Marine Corps O-1C Observation plane officially nicknamed the 'Bird Dog'. It had initially entered Marine Corps and US Army service in the 1950s. It performed a wide variety of roles such as target acquisition for artillery units and liaison work as well as a forward air control (FAC) aircraft supplementing the jet-powered versions. (*USMC*)

(**Opposite, above**) The Marine Corps' replacement for the O-1 Bird Dog would be the OV-10A, officially nick-named the 'Bronco'. Its official designation when initially conceived in 1962 was 'light armed-reconnaissance aircraft' with the first production example arriving in South Vietnam in July 1968. The USAF and US Navy would also employ the aircraft during the Vietnam War. (*USMC*)

(**Opposite, below**) The Marines pictured here are examining captured enemy weapons. On the right-hand side of the picture, a Marine is holding a 7.62mm AK-47 with the Marine on the left-hand side of the photograph clutching a Soviet-designed 7.62mm RPD light machine gun. The Marine in the centre is wearing the new camouflage tropical uniform introduced in late 1968. (*USMC*)

(**Opposite, above**) For the III MAF, the beginning of 1968 had been a momentous one with the extended seventy-seven-day siege of the KSCB that ran into early April 1968. It was followed by the massive Tet Offensive that began on 31 January 1968 and continued into early March of that year. The enemy did not let up and in May 1968 launched a 'Mini-Tet' with Marines in continuous combat throughout I Corps. (*USMC*)

(**Opposite, below**) One of the lesser-known fighting vehicles deployed by the Marine Corps during the Vietnam War was the XM733 pictured here. Developed from the standard M116 marginal terrain vehicle, the Marine Corps ordered ninety-three of them as an amphibious assault vehicle armed with a .50 calibre machine gun. This XM733 has an experimental Aerojet XM174 40mm grenade-launcher. (*USMC*)

(**Above**) The Marine riflemen pictured here are carrying away captured enemy 12.7mm machine guns. Draped over the chests of the two Marines in the foreground are cotton bandoliers containing twenty-round magazines for M16 rifles. Marine infantrymen in South Vietnam tended to dislike their uniform accoutrements and often traded for those used by the US Army and ARVN infantrymen. (*USMC*)

A Marine rifleman in South Vietnam has dispensed with the issued sling for his M16 rifle and replaced it with a makeshift example. Note that he does not have his flak jacket zipped up; doubtless because of the quick heat build-up it created. On the other hand, such a practice badly reduced the amount of protection it offered. (*USMC*)

A Marine examines his flak vest that deflected a possible bullet fragment. The first six months of 1968 proved the costliest of the Vietnam War for the Marine Corps, accounting for almost one-quarter of all those killed during the conflict. In those six months, 3,339 Marines died. During that period the 3d Division averaged about 220 killed per month and another 1,250 wounded per month. (*USMC*)

The very high loss rate of lower-ranking Marine riflemen in the first few months was of great concern to General Cushman, the commander of the III MAF. He informed the 1st and 3d divisions' commanders in May 1968 that 'we are suffering too many Marine casualties – particularly KIA [killed in action].' He attributed that to a misplaced reliance on 'do-or-die assaults'. (USMC)

General Cushman emphasized to his divisional commanders in May 1968 that more reliance be placed upon the support arms such as artillery and air support to reduce casualties. In response, the commandant of the Marine Corps felt that such a change in war fighting 'could lead to a degradation and even the loss' of the Marine Corps' traditional "can-do" offensive spirit'. (USMC)

A Marine rifleman appears here with a captured enemy soldier who is being questioned by an ARVN interpreter. The flurry of concern over the very high losses incurred by the Marines from January to May 1968 in South Vietnam became less of an issue beginning in June 1968 due to the inaction of the NVA from June 1968 to most of August 1968. *(USMC)*

On 24 August 1968, the enemy mounted the third of their Tet Offensives by firing upon twenty-seven different military installations and South Vietnamese cities. Their primary target would be the Da Nang air base, but their attacks were beaten off. Pictured here is a Marine with an M60 machine gun slung across his shoulder. (*USMC*)

On 5 November 1968 Richard Nixon, pictured here, won the American election for the office of president. He ran on a platform of ending the war in Vietnam as public opinion in the country was then heavily against continued involvement. How he planned to end the war in South-East Asia he did not divulge. Nixon assumed the office of president on 20 January 1969. (*DOD*)

Chapter Four

Coming to an End (1969–75)

On taking office in January 1969, President Nixon swiftly concluded that there would be no quick negotiated end to the Vietnam War. The only option at that point was a gradual hand over of the conduct of the war to the ARVN in a process labelled 'Vietnamization', a policy that had failed for the French in the 1950s. American military forces would be withdrawn in stages, as the ARVN gradually took over the fighting.

When Vietnamization began in early 1969, everybody knew it would not happen overnight. The III MAF would, therefore, continue search-and-destroy operations in the unpopulated northern hinterlands of I Corps to keep the enemy from massing their forces. In populated areas, the term 'cordon and search' would be applied.

Another continuing goal for the 1st Marine Division in 1969 would be the securing and pacification of as much of I Corps' populated coastal regions as possible. The objective would be the eventual handing over of its security to the ARVN. From an III MAP report outlining its plans for 1969 appears the following passage: 'Operations to annihilate the enemy, while clearly essential to pacification, are by themselves inadequate. The people must be separated and won over from the enemy.'

Change is in the Air

The operations conducted by the 3d Marine Division in the northern I Corps during the early part of 1969 did not come without cost, with 130 Marines killed and 920 wounded. According to the Marines, they accounted for 1,617 enemy dead and the seizure of a massive amount of supplies. In conjunction with ARVN units and US Army units, the Marines of the 3d Division continued in pursuit of enemy units and supply bases in northern I Corps until the summer of 1969.

In March 1969, Melvin R. Laird, President Nixon's Secretary of Defense, visited South Vietnam on a fact-finding mission. Based on his quick visit to the country, he concluded that Vietnamization was already going so well that up to 50,000 American military personnel could be withdrawn from South Vietnam by late 1969, with more the following year.

Laird's positive spin on Vietnamization was for American public consumption. He knew, as did others at senior levels of the US government and military, that the ARVN had no chance of success against the NVA/VC when American military forces finally withdrew. That information appeared in the National Security Memorandum No. 1, dated 1 February 1969, as seen in the following extracts from that document:

> The RVNAF alone cannot now, or in the foreseeable future, stand up to the current North Vietnamese-Vietcong forces … The enemy have suffered some reverses but they have not changed their essential objectives and they have sufficient strength to pursue these objectives. We are not attriting his forces faster than he can recruit or infiltrate.

Who Goes First?

The MACV selected for initial reassignment both a US Army division and the 3d Marine Division. Rather than pulling out all their men and equipment at the same time, these divisions would depart from South Vietnam in two phases.

General Abrams, the commander of the MACV, explained his reasoning for selecting the Marine division: 'Because it could go to Okinawa; because it would be leaving the area to the 1st ARVN Division, recognized by all as the strongest and best ARVN division; and finally, because northern I Corps has one of the best security environments in the country for the people.'

The commanders of the III MAF and FMF/Pac were a bit miffed that General Abrams scheduled no Marine aviation units for redeployment to Okinawa. In the end, some aviation elements of the 1st MAW did return to Okinawa with the 3d Marine Division, if only for training purposes.

The first elements of the Marine 3d Division departed South Vietnam on 15 June 1969, the last five months later on 24 November 1969. The first Marine aviation unit to leave South Vietnam by both air and sea began on 13 August 1969.

Redeployment Speed-Up

In early June 1969, Nixon signalled his desire to see further troop reductions, stating that he would decide on the matter in August 1969. Former Secretary of Defense Clark Clifford proposed, in a magazine article that summer, the withdrawal of 100,000 troops by the end of 1969 and the remainder the following year.

A Terrible Milestone

On 3 April 1969, the MACV officially acknowledged that more American military personnel had been killed up to that point in the Vietnam War than in the Korean War of 1950 to 1953. In the latter, 33,629 were killed and in the former 33,641 had died by that date.

Following a consultation with the American Joint Chiefs of Staff, President Nixon addressed the American public via a television broadcast on 16 September 1969. He informed them that the planned pull-out of 50,000 men from South Vietnam by the end of 1969 would be increased by 20 per cent to 60,000.

On the evening of 3 November 1969, Nixon once again went on television to announce to the American public a non-specific deadline for further pull-out of American military personnel: 'This withdrawal will be made from strength and not from weakness. As South Vietnamese forces become stronger, the rate of American withdrawal can become greater.'

Nixon announced on 15 December 1969 that he wanted 50,000 additional troops pulled from South Vietnam by 15 April 1970. Of that number, 12,900 would be Marines. The Marine Corps commandant at the time, General Leonard F. Chapman Jr, remembered: 'I felt, and I think that most Marines felt, that the time had come to get out of Vietnam.'

A Very Different War

While the 3d Marine Division, operating in the unpopulated northernmost province of I Corps, fought a mainly conventional war against NVA divisions until its departure, the opposite would be true of the 1st Marine Division defending southern I Corps. Within their zone of operation were the western mountains that the NVA had to transit before threatening the Da Nang air base and I Corps' densely populated coastal regions.

Colonel Robert H. Barrows recalled in a 1987 interview by the Marine Corps Historical Center how difficult it was for the men of the 1st Marine Division throughout 1969:

Those Marines who went out day after day conducting … combat patrols, almost knowing that somewhere on their route of movement, they were going to have some sort of surprise visited on them, either an ambush or explosive device … I think that is the worst kind of warfare, not being able to see the enemy. You can't shoot back at them. You are kind of helpless.

Lance Corporal Lester W. Weber's response to not being able to get to grips with an often-elusive enemy appears in an extract from his Medal of Honor citation. The date is 23 February 1969, and when his platoon came under heavy fire from concealed enemy soldiers he sprang into action:

He reacted by plunging into the tall grass, successfully attacking one enemy and forcing eleven others to break contact. Upon encountering a second North Vietnamese Army soldier, he overwhelmed him in fierce hand-to-hand combat. Observing two other soldiers firing upon his comrades from behind a dike,

Lance Corporal Weber ignored the frenzied firing of the enemy and, racing across the hazardous area, dived into their position. He neutralized the position by wrestling weapons from the hands of the two soldiers and overcoming them … As he moved forward to attack a fifth enemy soldier, he was mortally wounded.

Mines and Booby Traps

For the men of the 1st Marine Division on constant patrol, mines and booby traps set by the enemy took a heavy psychological toll. Colonel Charles S. Robertson noted in a Marine Historical Center interview, 'the bulk of casualties resulted from the abundance of surprise firing devices' instead of engagements with enemy forces.

Lieutenant Colonel Godfrey S. Delcuze noted in a July 1978 interview:

> The war had moved on except for sporadic, murderous local force mining. Brave men died 'pacifying' old men, women and children who refused to be pacified … They – the peasants – wreaked their havoc from time to time with M16 bouncing mines from fields US Forces had laid. The only identifiable 'military' service was a two-day lay-out ambush. The ambush netted one enemy soldier. He came walking down a trail with an M16 bouncing mine in each hand. We shot him in the gut. He was a 12-year-old boy.

To deal with the threat faced by Marines of the 1st Division from mines and booby traps, the division employed many different methods to reduce losses. These included bombarding with artillery and napalm the areas to be searched before the Marines' arrival. Once on site, the Marines would conduct the majority of their movements whenever possible mounted on armoured tracked vehicles. If forced to advance on foot, maximum dispersion was stressed to prevent a single mine or booby trap from killing or wounding more than one Marine at a time.

From a US Army manual titled *Booby Traps* issued in September 1965 is this extract describing their purpose: 'Booby traps supplement minefields by increasing their obstacle value … cause uncertainty and suspicion in the mind of the enemy. They may surprise him, frustrate his plans, and inspire in his soldiers a fear of the unknown.' Some 11 per cent of American deaths during the Vietnam War were attributed to enemy mines and booby traps, with another 17 per cent wounded by the devices.

The Countryside is the Enemy

In spite of continuous patrolling by the Marines of the 1st Division during the first six months of 1969, it proved impossible to stop small-scale enemy attacks on both Marine and civilian targets. To curtail this problem, the 1st Marine Division would mount even more small and large-scale operations in the last six months of 1969.

Not counting the threat from the enemy, both the terrain and climate of South Vietnam often proved to be a hardship for Marines. Lieutenant Colonel Ray Kummerow commented in a 1983 Marine Corps Historical Center interview:

[It] was 'billy goat'-type scramble from peak to peak, trying to maintain communications and cover of supporting arms … We were surprised at the casualties sustained from malaria and other diseases after a month of continuous fighting in that environment. The battalion dwindled to half field strength. India Company lost all its officers save the company commander … who requested relief because of fatigue.

What does 1970 have in Store?

By the end of 1969, approximately 55,000 Marines remained under III MAF control in South Vietnam. Of that number, 28,000 belonged to the 1st Marine Division. With the redeployment of some of its assets beginning in January 1970, by March of 1970 it would drop to only 21,000 personnel.

The main job for the remaining units of the 1st Marine Division in 1970 would be the continuation of the security and pacification activities from the previous year. Also, it would continue to assist in the process of Vietnamization and preparing itself for the orderly withdrawal of additional elements of the division from South Vietnam. The then commandant of the Marine Corps stated: 'Don't leave anything behind worth more than five dollars.'

Did the effort that the III MAF put into pacification ever have any chance of success? Some Marine senior officers touted its success. Lieutenant General McCutcheon of the III MAF stated in 1970 that despite 'improved ratings in the Hamlet Evaluation system', the majority of the rural population of South Vietnam remained equally 'apathetic' to their own government or to the enemy, and considered the Vietnamization process as 'a euphemism for US withdrawal'.

The 12,900 Marines planned to be withdrawn from South Vietnam by 15 April 1970; as Nixon ordered, they would end their combat operations beginning in late January 1970. With their departure, US Army personnel in I Corps exceeded the number of Marines. The result was that the III MAF became subordinate to the US Army XXIV Corps command on 9 March 1970.

Operations in the 1970s

With the continuing drawdown of the 1st Marine Division, large-scale battalion-sized and larger operations became far less common. When the Marines did venture out in force to search for enemy base camps, their efforts did not always have the desired effect. The enemy had learned, when given the opportunity, to build more base camps than they required to offset those destroyed during Marine search-and-destroy operations.

An enemy defector stated:

The people in the base camp do not worry about allied operations. Forewarning of an attack is obvious at the base camp when FWMAF [Free World Military Armed Forces] conduct air strikes, artillery fire, aerial reconnaissance, and when helicopters fly in the area. When an operation takes place in the vicinity of the base camp, the people simply go further back into the mountains and return when the operation is over.

In the endless patrols by the 1st Division Marines during the first six months of 1970, individual Marines continued to perform acts of incredible bravery. On 8 May 1970, machine-gunner Lance Corporal Miguel Keith's platoon came under attack by a superior enemy force. Despite being wounded in the initial barrage of enemy fire, he continued to fire upon them. In an extract from his Medal of Honor citation we see what then transpired:

At this point, a grenade detonated near Lance Corporal Keith, knocking him to the ground and inflicting further severe wounds. Fighting pain and weakness from loss of blood, he again braved the concentrated hostile fire to charge an

---

Anarchy in the Ranks

With the end of America's involvement in the Vietnam War in sight and nobody wanting to be the last man killed, Marine morale began to slide. The decreased morale resulted in a host of issues including a breakdown in discipline and increased drug abuse by Marines. Senior officers believed that by 1970 some-where between 30 and 50 per cent of their men had some involvement with drugs. To make up for the high losses suffered by the Marine Corps in the Vietnam War, recruitment standards had been lowered and training shortened.

Another grave issue was violence among the ranks, such as whites against blacks. These incidents included large-scale race riots, both on Marine bases in South Vietnam and in the United States. On a smaller scale, the white v. black confrontations included individual fights, muggings and even robberies. However, in the field the problem was not nearly as serious as all faced a common enemy.

An additional issue revolved around the growing degree of violence between enlisted men and their officers. In a Marine Corps Historical Center publication Colonel Robert H. Barrow stated: 'This war has produced one form of felony that no other war has ever had; more despicable and inexplicable thing [than] in any other wars that I have ever seen ... And that is the felonious attack of one Marine against another, very often with a hand grenade ... I don't think anybody ever recalls some officers or some NCO being killed in combat by his own troops intentionally. In Vietnam, yes. We had several of these.'

estimated twenty-five enemy soldiers who were massing to attack. The vigor of his assault and his well-placed fire eliminated four of the enemy while the remainder fled for cover. During this valiant effort, he was mortally wounded by an enemy soldier.

To show that neither the ARVN nor the Marines could protect them within I Corps, VC main force units attacked two pro-South Vietnamese villages on 11 June 1970. At the first, they killed seventy-four and wounded many others. In the second they killed 150 civilians and injured another 60. A Marine recalled:

> The enemy ran through the village, ordering people out of their bunkers. When they did [come out], they were shot, or else [the enemy threw] chicoms [grenades] into the bunker, killing the men, women, and children in them … Very many civilians [were] killed just inside their bunkers, if it wasn't from shrapnel wounds it was from fire where they were burned to death from the satchel charges used.

As in the past, the results of the various operations undertaken by the 1st Marine Division during the first six months of 1970 proved hard to measure. The enemy tended to avoid any large-scale activities during that time and merely sought to inflict on the Marines as many casualties as possible with minimal effort. The Marines were therefore engaged in what had become a slow, bloody war of attrition. They claimed 3,955 enemy dead for the loss of 283 killed and 2,537 wounded during that period.

The Last Six Months

In spite of its ever-reducing numbers, the 1st Marine Division continued with offensive operations in the latter part of 1970. The last major operation of the division received the name IMPERIAL LAKE and would be in conjunction with both US Army and ARVN units. The operation began on 1 September 1970, and ran until May 1971 with the goal of clearing an enemy-occupied area located 20 miles south of the Da Nang air base.

As the Marines uncovered enemy base camps and tunnels during Operation IMPERIAL LAKE, according to a Marine Corps Historical Center publication: 'They blew up the structures with plastic explosive and seeded caves with crystallized CS

The Unwilling

In April 1970, the Marines announced that they would stop taking draftees; something they had never been comfortable doing but it had become necessary due to a lack of sufficient volunteers. In total, the Marine Corps took in 42,000 draftees during the Vietnam War.

riot gas. If the enemy reoccupied a seeded cave, the heat from their bodies and from lamps or cooking fires would cause the CS to resume its gaseous state, and render the cave uninhabitable.'

By 1 September 1970, the III MAF had dropped to 24,527 personnel, with around 12,500 belonging to the 1st Marine Division. The remaining Marines were spared heavy combat with the enemy during the year's last four months. Some thought that poor weather conditions and extensive flooding had curtailed enemy offensive operations. For the Marines, this proved a fortunate event as it forced the usually hidden enemy to the surface. In some locations they were quickly spotted and eliminated.

What's Going On?

Major John S. Grinalds, the intelligence officer (S-2) of the 1st Marine Division, had a different view on the lack of enemy activity during the latter part of 1970. He believed that the enemy had a master plan which involved allowing the American military to withdraw from South Vietnam mostly unhindered, with just enough activity to remind both the South Vietnamese and American public that the war remained in effect, but not enough to be seen as a significant threat that might cause the American military to slow down withdrawal from the country.

Major Grinalds would go on to later state that he 'expected the enemy to bide their time, building up their supply stockpiles, and recruit more guerrillas and VCI [VC infrastructure] members, while they weakened civilian confidence in the South Vietnamese government by continued terrorism and propaganda'. Then, as Grinalds put it, 'in July [1971], when we finally stepped out, they could come in with their main force units and either act politically or militarily to … control the area.'

Vietnamization Issues

The high-minded goals of Vietnamization that allowed the 1st Marine Division to depart from South Vietnam eventually left the security of the country in theory in the well-prepared hands of the ARVN and its various types of militia units. That was not to be possible for myriad reasons. These included the complex web of political ties among the South Vietnamese military elite that ran the country, meaning that personal loyalty typically counted more than military competence in achieving rank.

A Marine general complained in August 1970 that the ARVN senior leadership had 'little appreciation for the time and space factors involved in an operation, nor of the logistic effort required to support one'. An example of the ARVN's sometimes indifferent attitude to Marine efforts on their country's behalf would be the well-equipped and highly-trained units they were operating near the Da Nang air base in 1970. A Marine officer recalled that 'they [the ARVN] never provided any support to anyone within the area immediately around Da Nang.'

At the lower scale of operations, those Marines involved in small unit security and pacification roles at the village level often found that the ARVN militia units would not always be around when the fighting started. A Marine corporal recalled

> that initially in night firefights … you'd look around and … there wouldn't be no PFs [Popular Force militiamen] there. They'd be hiding behind gullies, bushes, trees, anything you could find down on the ground, in a hole. After a while they'd see that we was getting up, was going into it. Course you had every once in a while to knock a few heads and put a few rounds over the top of 'em, but they finally got to where they started to go with us.

By the end of 1970, Marines at the local levels had improved some of the ARVN militia units. They would sometimes even mount offensive actions against local enemy units. However, the Marines who worked with them commented that the militia leadership failed to grasp that to be successful at deterring the enemy from attacking they had to keep continuous pressure on the enemy and should not immediately withdraw to their fortified camps upon the conclusion of offensive actions.

A Deeper Problem

American advisers had moulded the ARVN in the image of the US Army. Superficially it presented a facade of strength, possessing many of the trappings expected of a modern army such as tanks or artillery. However, behind the facade, it lacked a suitable logistic infrastructure or the trained specialists and equipment that kept the American military up and running.

Most serious among the ARVN's shortfalls were those of their fixed-wing or helicopter assets. The MACV would be fully aware of this issue, but given the timetable imposed by Nixon for the American military withdrawal from South Vietnam, not much could be done to rectify it in time.

Big Changes Take Place

On the first day of 1971, the relationship between the local ARVN forces and the Marine 1st Division changed. The former now had full responsibility for the security of the countryside. The latter, reflecting their ever-dwindling numbers, were now tasked primarily with the protection of the Da Nang air base, although two infantry regiments of the 1st Marine Division remained in the field for the time being.

By early April 1971, only a single regiment of the 1st Marine Division remained in South Vietnam. Their orders stressed that if they encountered a superior enemy force they were to withdraw and allow artillery to deal with them. On 14 April 1971, the III MAF relocated to Okinawa. Command of the last Marine ground troops in South Vietnam passed the same day to the just-activated 3d Marine Amphibious Brigade (MAB).

Getting There

The last search-and-destroy operation conducted by the men of the 1st Marine Division bore the name Operation SCOTT ORCHARD. It began on 7 April and ended on 11 April 1971, with no losses for the Marines. On 11 April 1971, Nixon welcomed home the initial elements of the 1st Marine Division at Camp Pendleton, located in Southern California.

On 7 May 1971, Operation IMPERIAL LAKE concluded. It had lasted eight months and had cost the Marines 24 dead and 170 wounded. The Marines claimed at least 300 enemy dead in exchange. On the same day that Operation IMPERIAL LAKE ended, the Marine Corps ceased all ground combat operations in South Vietnam.

All Marine Corps security and pacification efforts were turned over to the ARVN on 11 May 1971. By this point, the resentment of the South Vietnamese (both military and civilian) had become a serious problem as they felt they were being abandoned by the United States. In some incidents they threatened and even fired their weapons at Marines.

In a Marine Corps Historical Center publication appears this statement from the senior province advisor within the I Corps area on 3 March 1971: 'Anti-foreign [American] feeling continues at an endemic level. Incidents are becoming more numerous and testy … Further increases can be expected as opportunists will use incidents to further nefarious ends.'

On 26 May 1971, the last Marine air combat unit departed from South Vietnam. The 3d MAB turned over to the US Army the last piece of ground under its control on 4 June and closed its headquarters on 26 June. It deactivated on the following day.

The only ground force Marines remaining in South Vietnam at the end of June 1971 were approximately 500 men assigned to liaison and advisory duties. They began leaving the country in March 1973, much to the consternation of the ARVN. At that point the only remaining Marine ground troops in South Vietnam were 143 men assigned to guard the American Embassy in Saigon.

The Toll

During the Marine Corps' time in South Vietnam from 1965 till 1973, more than 500,000 Marines had spent some time in the country. Of those who served, 13,005 had died and another 88,635 were wounded. The Vietnam War Memorial in Washington DC, however, lists 14,809 Marine dead during the Vietnam War. These losses were higher than those sustained by the Marine Corps during the Second World War. Those came to 25,511 dead and 68,207 wounded. Improvements in medical care helped to keep down the count of Marine dead during the Vietnam War.

The Closing Acts

On 30 March 1972, the NVA launched their Easter Offensive aimed at the over-throw of the South Vietnamese government. To provide much-needed aerial support for the ARVN, the American government committed a number of Marine air combat squadrons, which flew out of the Da Nang air base and Thailand.

The US Navy and Air Force also contributed assets to the fight. With that air support, the ARVN managed to turn back the enemy offensive by 22 October 1972. The last Marine air combat squadrons had departed South-East Asia the month before on 1 September 1972.

The last Marine embassy guards left South Vietnam by helicopter with the fall of the country's government on 30 April 1975. The NVA offensive that led to the end of the Vietnam War had begun the previous month and had quickly overwhelmed the ARVN, which had been denied American air power this time around. The reason was that the American public and its political representatives in Congress had wanted no more involvement in the long-running conflict, knowing that the South Vietnamese government was doomed.

A Marine Corps military police bunker guarding one of the roads leading to the Da Nang air base. At the beginning of 1969, the III MAF under the command of General Robert E. Cushman consisted of approximately 81,000 Marines roughly divided among the 1st and 3d Marine divisions and supporting troops. There were another 15,500 men that made up the 1st MAW that also came under the oversight of the III MAF. (*USMC*)

On 26 March 1969, Lieutenant General Herman Nickerson, Jr, pictured here, replaced General Robert E. Cushman as commander of the III MAF. Like all the other senior-ranking generals of the Vietnam War era, he was a much-decorated veteran of both the Second World War and the Korean War. He had served as the commander of the 3d Marine Division from October 1966 to May 1967. (*USMC*)

An M109 155mm self-propelled artillery howitzer in a secure rear area, based on the posture of the Marine crew. Besides all its Marine units, the III MAF also oversaw approximately 50,000 US Army personnel within the I Corps Tactical Area of Responsibility (TAOR) in 1969. The US Army units had been transferred to command of the III MAF the previous year by the MACV. (*USMC*)

On 17 April 1969, the US Army in South Vietnam transferred some of its M107 175mm self-propelled guns as seen here to the III MAF. They were the intended replacements for three M53 155mm self-propelled gun batteries. All of the artillery assets of the 1st Marine Division fell under the command of the 11th Marine Regiment and those of the 3d Marine Division under the 12th Marine Regiment. (*USMC*)

(**Above**) The Marine M110 8in self-propelled howitzer pictured here in South Vietnam and the M107 175mm self-propelled gun were mounted onto the same low-profile tracked chassis. That chassis received power from a diesel engine. The only armour protection on the vehicle existed for the driver who resided in the left front side of the vehicle with the engine located to his right. (*USMC*)

(**Opposite, above**) The combined strength of the 11th and 12th regiments in 1969 came in at 242 howitzers, guns and 4.2in (107mm) mortars. The most numerous divisional towed artillery piece throughout the Marine Corps' involvement in the Vietnam War would be the Second World War-era M101A1 105mm towed howitzer pictured here. (*USMC*)

(**Opposite, below**) The main mission for Marine Corps' artillery in the Vietnam War would be to provide fire in support of offensive operation and defensive operations. Besides providing fire support for the Marine units if called upon, the 11th and 12th Marine regiments would answer calls for fire support from US Army units as well as ARVN units. In addition, they would sometimes be called upon to fire their weapons in support of the South Korean Marine units that served during the conflict. (*USMC*)

Here a Marine is loading an HE (high-explosive) round into the breech of the 155mm howitzer found on the M109 self-propelled howitzer. Marine artillery regiments were often called upon to prepare landing zones and fire support bases for friendly occupation by blasting away vegetation for helicopters to land. These fire missions would often entail a minimum of 1,000 rounds of ammunition. (*USMC*)

(**Opposite, above**) Seen here in full recoil is the barrel of a Marine M114A1 155mm towed howitzer. A common fire mission would be in the suppression role, engaging suspected enemy bases as well as artillery, rocket or mortar sites. These missions went by the names 'unobserved', 'harassing' or 'interdiction' fires. They were initiated by specific intelligence from informants, radar or even radio intercepts. (*USMC*)

(**Opposite, below**) In January 1969, the III MAF had a total of 258 fixed-wing aircraft such as the A-4 Skyhawks pictured here and 270 helicopters. Most of the fixed-wing Marine aircraft flew out of the Da Nang air base. By way of comparison, the MACV had under its control approximately 740 fixed-wing aircraft mostly from the USAF and about 3,400 helicopters, the majority belonging to the US Army. (*USMC*)

The terrain and weather of South Vietnam often made it difficult to see the enemy or determine the effectiveness of aircraft sorties. Poor weather conditions or night-time sorties often called for the use of an Air Support Radar Team (ASRT) which vectored aircraft, such as the A-6 Intruder shown here, to their targets with input from seismic and acoustic ground sensors. (*USMC*)

An F-4 Phantom II of the 1st MAW with a full bomb load. At first, Marine pilots dropped their bombs from lower than 200ft for the best accuracy. However, this would eventually be increased to a minimum of 300ft for safety reasons to prevent fixed-wing aircraft finding themselves caught in the explosions of their own bombs at low levels. The US Navy developed bomb-retarding kits that accordingly came into use with the 1st MAW. (*USMC*)

Besides large numbers of enemy anti-aircraft guns (both optical and radar-guided) of different calibres posing a threat to the aircraft of the 1st MAW, a new threat appeared possibly as early as 1968. That was the Soviet-designed and supplied 9K32 Strela-2 surface-to-air anti-aircraft missile seen here in the hands of an NVA soldier. To the American military, it was known as the SA-7 Grail. (*USMC*)

(**Above**) In this picture we see ARVN soldiers and their advisers rushing supplies out of a Marine UH-34 helicopter, no doubt under enemy fire. The piston-engine-powered UH-34 helicopter would finally be retired from service in South Vietnam in early August 1969. From 1965 until 1969 they flew over 917,000 sorties, and were replaced by the CH-46 Sea Knight and the CH-53 Sea Stallion. (*USMC*)

(**Opposite, above**) In 1969, the first examples of the improved CH-46D model Sea Knight helicopters arrived in South Vietnam to replace the earlier trouble-plagued CH-46A version. All of the existing examples of the latter would be eventually upgraded to the 'D' model standard. With a more powerful engine, the later model of the Sea Knight could lift 2,720lb whereas the older model was limited to 1,710lb under combat conditions. (*USMC*)

(**Opposite, below**) A view inside a Marine CH-46 Sea Knight helicopter during the Vietnam War. From a 1969 Marine report on helicopters' use appears this passage: 'Viewing the nature of the war, the terrain, and the enemy … we never had enough helicopters to satisfy the needs and requirements of the two divisions.' The resulting overuse of the existing helicopters therefore greatly shortened their intended service lives. (*USMC*)

(**Above**) The CH-46 Sea Knight typically had two .50 calibre machine guns for self-defence. The helicopters of the 1st MAW during the first six months of 1969 were flying between 47,000 to a high in April 1969 of 52,000 sorties a month. One of the problems that resulted from these high sortie rates was an excessive incidence of pilot fatigue that in turn raised the accident rate. (*USMC*)

(**Opposite, above**) On 10 April 1969, the first of twenty-four AH-1G Cobra gunships as seen here arrived in South Vietnam. The tandem-seat dedicated helicopter gunship carried an array of weapons ranging from 40mm grenade-launchers to 2.75in rockets. It was the replacement for the UH-1E Huey in the gunship role. The UH-1E then reverted to its original role as an observation platform. (*USMC*)

(**Opposite, below left**) In the name of pacification, beginning in late 1965, the Marines had a project referred to as the Combined Action Programme (CAP). It consisted of a rifle squad of Marines and a US Navy corpsman assigned to assist a local South Vietnamese militia unit in defence of its village. The Marines involved in the programme came to be known as Combined Action Platoons (CAPs). Pictured here is a patrol of local militia members. (*USMC*)

(**Opposite, below right**) The III MAF put into the field Mobile Training Teams (MTTs) to improve the combat effectiveness of South Vietnamese militia units in villages that did not have a CAP in place. The militia member in the foreground is armed with an M1 Garand rifle. The M1 Garand, and the M1 and M2 American-designed and built carbines, were standard equipment for the ARVN until replacement by the M16 rifle. (*USMC*)

In early 1969, the American military put the enemy personnel count in South Vietnam at approximately 73,000 men. These were broken down into 42,700 NVA, another 6,500 main force VC and local force unit members with some 23,500 guerrillas. Also there was a 16,000 political and quasi-military cadre. Pictured here is what appears to be a Viet Cong main force unit planning an attack by using a model of their target. (USMC)

A Marine rifleman checks for booby traps on the corpse of what is likely a Viet Cong guerrilla, based on the fact that he has either an M1 or M2 carbine. As that weapon went to the ARVN and its militia units in large numbers, it could be a captured example. Others were stolen from supply ships or arms warehouses by South Vietnamese civilian workers. (USMC)

The NVA soldiers seen here tended to be better-armed and trained than their VC main force counterparts. Heavy losses incurred by the Viet Cong main force units led to their replacement in many units with NVA soldiers, a practice that had begun as early as 1964. Despite the ever-rising number of NVA soldiers in many VC main force units, they retained their VC designation to make it appear that they were indigenous people. (USMC)

(**Above**) In this picture, we see American President Richard M. Nixon on the left and his Secretary of Defense Melvin Laird to the right. On 3 May 1969, Laird announced that the American military would soon begin troop withdrawals from South Vietnam if certain conditions came about in theatre. These included an improvement in the fighting ability of the ARVN and a major reduction in enemy activity. (*USMC*)

(**Opposite, above**) To provide a possible cover story on how American military forces could withdraw without the collapse of the South Vietnamese military, the term 'Vietnamization' would be put forward by Nixon's White House. It presumed the American military bringing the ARVN up to American performance standards. Pictured here is a Marine adviser instructing South Vietnamese Marines on the use of the 81mm mortar. (*USMC*)

(**Opposite, below**) On 12 May, the enemy struck throughout South Vietnam with the largest number of attacks since their initial Tet Offensive in January 1968. In spite of these activities, the decision to withdraw American troops remained in place. On 8 June 1969, President Nixon announced that by the end of August 1969 another 25,000 American military personnel would withdraw from South Vietnam. (*USMC*)

Despite the declared drawdown of American military forces, the III MAF continued with an endless series of operations to deter the enemy's plans. These operations included constant patrolling to find the enemy, as seen here. The Marine rifleman in the foreground is carrying an M79 grenade-launcher and wearing an ammo vest with pouches to store 40mm rounds. (*USMC*)

A Marine rifleman and his scout dog take a break from patrolling. The enemy also employed scout dogs on occasion to locate Marine infantrymen. On 13 August 1969, the first major unit of the 1st MAW, a medium helicopter squadron, departed from South Vietnam. The squadron had been the first to arrive in South Vietnam in April 1962. (*USMC*)

Even as the process of withdrawing Marines and other American military personnel began in early 1969, Marines continued to be attacked by the enemy in numerous engagements. The lucky Marine pictured here managed to avoid death when his helmet took a round. To remember that fortunate break, he had marked the date when the incident occurred. (*USMC*)

(**Above**) On patrol, Marine infantrymen look for enemy supplies or possibly the entrance to an enemy tunnel. In August 1969, additional Marine units began to withdraw from South Vietnam. President Nixon proclaimed on 16 September 1969 that another 40,500 men, including 18,400 Marines mostly from the 3d Division, would depart before the end of the year. (*USMC*)

(**Opposite, above**) When enemy tunnels were found, fearless volunteers nicknamed 'tunnel rats' would descend into them to find and dispose of those within. Pictured here is a Marine tunnel rat armed with a .45 automatic pistol exiting a tunnel. Normally when entering into the depths he would also carry a flashlight. Some of the enemy tunnels encountered during the conflict led to multi-level complexes. (*USMC*)

(**Opposite, below**) Shown are some of the items recovered by a Marine patrol from an enemy tunnel seen in the background. Visible is a Soviet Army helmet without a liner, and an 82mm mortar baseplate as well as some 82mm mortar rounds. Also visible are RPG warheads and a single mine. The minimum depth of enemy tunnels would be 4ft, with a few found as deep as 40ft. (*USMC*)

(**Above**) Throughout the Vietnam War, the enemy made widespread use of mines and booby traps. In this picture we see a Marine engineer team searching for the magnetic signal of a buried enemy mine with an electrical mine detector. The enemy had a wide range of mines from the Soviet Union and Red China, including anti-tank mines as well as anti-personnel mines. (*USMC*)

(**Opposite, above**) A Marine engineer is shown attempting to disarm an enemy mine. One of the first steps is carefully searching around and under the mine, locating and neutralizing all activation fuses. Mines are made safe by making the main fuse safe. Some anti-tank mines cannot be made safe, but as they require hundreds of pounds of pressure to detonate, they can be removed to a safe place and then destroyed. (*USMC*)

(**Opposite, below**) A Marine rifleman offers a wounded comrade a drink of water from his canteen. Every Marine in the field had a first-aid kit attached to the rear of his service belt. Its contents could differ, but typically held an assortment of bandages and medication for treating burns. The US Navy provided medical corpsmen to Marine infantry formations during the Vietnam War. (*USMC*)

A total of 88,635 Marines were wounded during the Vietnam War. In this photograph we see Marines rushing to place a wounded buddy onto a medical evacuation helicopter. Head wounds tended to be the most common for infantrymen and resulted in the highest death rate. Enemy mines and booby traps, even if they did not kill, often caused the loss of a limb or limbs. (USMC)

Crewmen on a Marine helicopter attend to a wounded Marine while in flight. Of those Marines killed during the Vietnam War, enemy small-arms fire accounted for 51 per cent of deaths and 16 per cent of wounded. Enemy artillery fire accounted for another 36 per cent of deaths and 65 per cent of wounded. Enemy mines and booby traps resulted in a 13 per cent death rate and 19 per cent of the wounded. (USMC)

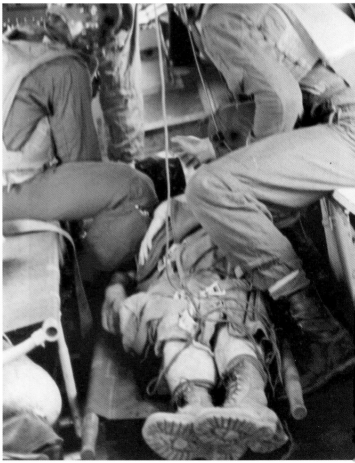

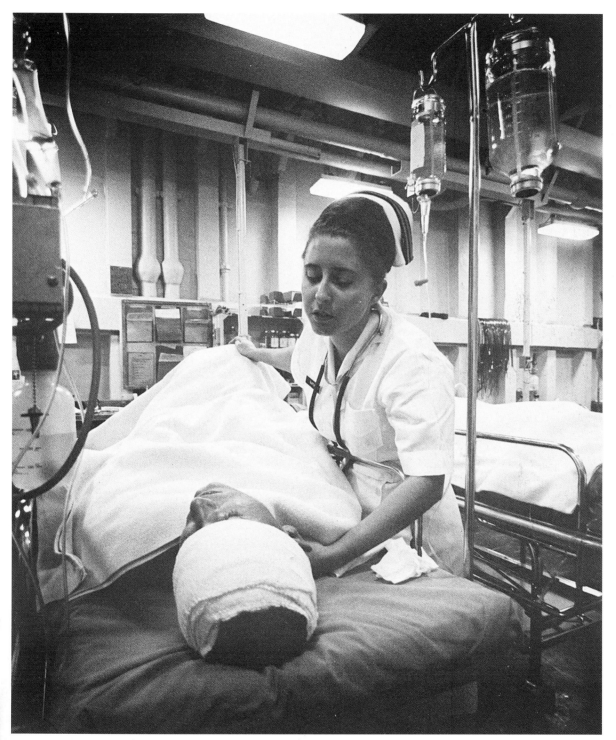

For the most seriously injured Marines, the next-to-last step in the medical evacuation process might be transfer to a hospital ship as seen here. With the latest in medical equipment and well-trained staff, such ships could perform any necessary medical procedures. Once stabilized, the patient might be flown Stateside to a military hospital. (*USMC*)

Members of a Marine reconnaissance unit are shown on patrol in South Vietnam in this photograph. Interesting is the beret on the Marine in the foreground, a not very common piece of headgear. That same Marine is wearing a non-standard camouflage uniform referred to as the 'duck hunter' scheme. (*USMC*)

A Marine scout-sniper team in action. On 15 December 1969, President Nixon announced that the third round of American military troop withdrawals from South Vietnam was to be completed by 15 April 1970. With the continued withdrawal of Marine units of the III MAF, their numbers by the end of 1969 were down to 54,559 men. (*USMC*)

Near the end of a major Marine Corps presence in South Vietnam, some Marines began to mark up their helmet covers as shown. In spite of the continued withdrawal of American military personnel beginning in 1969 going into 1970, the enemy did not reciprocate in accord with the terms of the cease-fire agreement between the American government and the North Vietnamese government. (*USMC*)

A Marine is shown here rushing out of a CH-46 Sea Knight helicopter. He is carrying a 60mm mortar over his shoulder. On 17 February 1969, President Nixon claimed that the military aspects of Vietnamization were proceeding on schedule, despite those at the most senior levels of the American government and military knowing that it was a falsehood. (*USMC*)

A young Marine takes cover on the battlefield. Beginning in 1969, with the drawdown of Marine numbers in South Vietnam, there began a process of deactivating some Marine units in both South Vietnam and the United States. In September 1969, the 5th Marine Division would be deactivated, reflecting a planned scaled-down post-Vietnam War Marine Corps. (*USMC*)

On 19 February 1970, with the continuing withdrawal of Marine units from South Vietnam, the US Army personnel in the I Corps TAOR outnumbered the Marines. This led to plans to place the III MAF under US Army oversight beginning on 9 March 1970. The 3d Marine Division had departed by December 1969, leaving only the 1st Marine Division in South Vietnam. (*USMC*)

(**Opposite, above**) In July 1970, the III MAF launched two major operations aimed at denying the enemy access to the latest rice harvest within I Corps. By this time large-scale engagements had become infrequent, although the enemy would constantly engage the remaining III MAF troops in a deadly war of ambushes, small battles, and rocket and mortar attacks. (*USMC*)

(**Opposite, below**) A Marine helicopter crewman points out the enemy bullet that lodged in his APH5 helmet. By the end of 1970, the 1st Marine Division in South Vietnam had shrunk to some 12,500 men. That same month President Nixon warned the North Vietnamese government that if they continued to increase the level of fighting in South Vietnam, he would resume bombing of North Vietnam. (*USMC*)

(**Above**) Military policemen stand guard with an M2 .50 calibre machine gun. On 6 January 1971, Secretary of Defense Laird stated that Vietnamization was running ahead of schedule and that combat missions for all American military personnel would end in the summer of 1972. On the down side, the NVA had begun bringing in more heavy artillery north of the DMZ. (*USMC*)

(**Above**) Marines leaving South Vietnam line up to board a US Navy ship. In early 1971, the III MAP was down to 24,700 men. The 1st MAW had only 74 fixed-wing aircraft remaining and 111 helicopters. In April 1971, the last elements of the 1st Marine Division left South Vietnam. That same month the III MAF Headquarters departed. The only formation remaining would be the 3d Marine Amphibious Force. (*USMC*)

(**Opposite, above**) During the redeployments from 1969 to 1971, Marine logisticians successfully withdrew vast quantities of equipment. They also dismantled many of their installations or turned them over to the ARVN. Those Marine installations dismantled came about as the ARVN lacked the personnel strength to maintain or staff them. Pictured here is a Marine checking to see if the load on a semi-truck is secured correctly. (*USMC*)

(**Opposite, below**) A Marine colour guard is furling its regimental flag before it departs by ship from South Vietnam. It's an apt moment reflecting the end of a significant Marine Corps presence in the country, except for some advisers and liaison personnel. On 4 June 1971, the 3d MAB turned over the last piece of real estate for which it had responsibility to the United States Army. (*USMC*)

Notes

Notes

Notes